WORD AND DOCTRINE

WORD AND DOCTRINE

by John W. Vannorsdall
Philip R. Hoh, Editor
Sidney Quinn, Artist
Lutheran Church Press
Philadelphia, Penna.

CONTENTS

introduction

Simplicity is not a virtue when it exists at the expense of the truth. The basic issues of human life can be stated simply, but they are never really simple, clear-cut, black-and-white. Even in our relations with one another we find our motivations mixed, our course of action uncertain. How much more complex, then, is our relationship to God, and how much more difficult and far-reaching are our attempts to explain that relationship to other men. The Christian faith can be stated simply, and this is usually the way in which it has first come to us. But as we grow older we find that it is not really simple at all.

There is, for example, the question concerning Christian doctrine: Are the doctrines of our particular denomination the truth? The answer is, of course, yes. And yet, it is also possible to answer in the negative without rejecting the doctrine. For our doctrines are not the truth in the sense in which God is Truth. Doctrines are, after all, the formulations of men, and men are fallible. So far as our understanding takes us, we confess that they reflect the truth of God's disclosure of himself in Jesus Christ. Yet, they are *our* formulations, and therefore subject to error and the limitations of language. So we move from the simple assertion that the doctrines of the church are the truth to a restatement of the question: In what sense are doctrinal statements to be considered true? The simplicity of our first question and answer is lost, but the question and response which replace it are doors which open to new meaning and insight.

So often the questions and answers of our youth become barriers to our later growth in understanding. For example, we are taught that the Bible comes to us from God. And then we learn that there are matters in the Bible which are contradicted by historians or scientists. This leads some people to conclude that the whole Bible must be in error and therefore of no value. But this is to ignore the more profound truth which the church confesses—that the Bible is God's gift to us and speaks the truth, while at the same time being a testimony of men and reflecting man's limitations.

A part of a Christian's growth is to understand that some of the questions which we once answered with a simple yes *or* no, must now be answered both yes *and* no, which means essentially that the question must be qualified or restated. This will not lead to greater simplicity, but it will drive us to examine more carefully the richness of Christian teaching.

Words and Life

In this course, teaching of the church is approached through a study of words which are central to its expression. Few of us would deny that such words as faith, justification, sin, grace, redemption, and death are basic to any discussion of Christianity, to say nothing of their importance to our worship. Yet the way in which these words are used among us varies tremendously. To some, faith means resolutely shutting our eyes to scientific fact. Others would describe faith as a form of knowledge. Some would say that it is something which man wills to do; others, that faith is a response won from us by God.

One of our first tasks, therefore, is to come as close as we can to understanding what the Jews meant when they spoke of sin and grace, of life and death. This is not to say that there was once a perfect understanding of these words which must somehow be recaptured. But Christianity does regard history as the arena in which God reveals himself, and biblical history is one of the clearer series of events and accounts.

For this reason it is important to know as clearly as possible what the Hebrews meant when they spoke of God in a particular way. We must also know what these words meant to our Lord and to his disciples. What did they mean to the church when the fathers used them in our creeds? What did they mean to Luther and Calvin at the time of the Reformation?

In this course, however, we are not interested in the development of words as such, but in understanding them well enough to speak and think intelligently about the life and teaching of the church today.

The Approach

In the discussion of each of the key words presented here, passages of Scripture which best show the biblical use of the word are quoted or cited. Wherever possible, references are made to Luther's *Small Catechism* and to the *Augsburg Confession* as indications of the way in which the concept was expressed at the time of the Reformation. In some instances, references are made to contemporary literature to illustrate the form which Christian teaching, or non-Christian teaching dealing with relevant problems, has found in our own time.

There are many ways of approach to Christian teaching. It is hoped that this study of key words will allow the reader a fresh and relevant way to study his response to the God who announces himself to us in Jesus Christ.

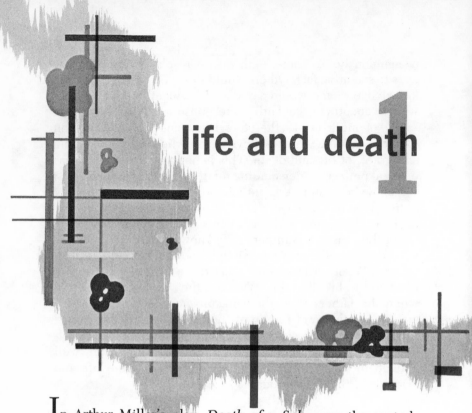

life and death

1

In Arthur Miller's play, *Death of a Salesman*, the central character, Willy Loman, kills himself. But the story is tragic not because of his death, but because both his life and his death were based on illusion. He had lost contact with reality and depended instead on fantasies of himself as a first-rate salesman, and of his sons achieving success on the basis of strength, good looks, and personality. His requiem is said by one of his sons: "He never knew who he was." This is the biblical meaning of death: to live by the wrong answer to the question of who we are—or never to have an answer at all.

Who Are We?

"—Then the Lord God formed man of dust from the ground, and breathed into his nostrils the breath of life; and man became a living being" (Genesis 2:7). For Jews and Christians, this is the sum and substance of who we are; it is the meaning of life and death.

Man is a creature and his creator is God. He has no origin within himself. He did not arise by chance. The life which he has is not his own, for he lives by the "breath of God."

There is no evidence, in the scientific sense of that word, for this witness concerning who we are. Biologists postulate that all things which we now call living have evolved out of basic chemical elements. This is not to say that we can no longer distinguish between things living and things not living, but it does mean that there is no basic discontinuity between the inanimate and the animate, and no basic discontinuity between animals and man. There are many missing links in the evolutionary chain, but many scientists see no need whatsoever for a special act of God to mark the progression from basic elements to man. In fact, they challenge us to point to any specific time and say, "Before this time man did not exist and after this time man did exist." They will show us, instead, periods of tens of thousands of years in which certain changes took place and within which it is purely arbitrary whether we call this particular form of life man or animal.

Neither is there much scientific evidence for the biblical understanding in our common and natural perception of things. A seed is planted, and usually grows into a plant; the plant produces seeds, and they are planted, and they grow. Some men will pray that their seeds grow and some men will not, but the seeds grow just the same. The human seed is planted and some will pray that a child be born, and some will not. Some men will pray for long life, and some men for death to come soon, but there seems to be no significant correlation between the prayers and the results. As with the seasons, birth and death follow a natural course with the generations rising and passing away. If God is a part of all of this, he seems to be imposed upon the natural process, and not essential to it.

There is a strong tradition among us that man has a soul which is immortal. We see that the body follows a natural

11

process of birth and life and death, but the soul is invisible, the seat of the real self, and the invisible soul continues to live beyond the death of the body. Some who hold this view are neither Jews nor Christians, but simply good men who cannot believe that the goodness of a man can really have an end. The roots of this view are in primitive animism which responds with awe to that which is wondrous and which attributes benevolent and malevolent spirits to what the natural eye sees. It is a view which received its sophisticated form in Plato, and its poetic expression in the romantic periods of more recent centuries. But this view, which at first seems to support the biblical view, is quite opposed to it. The biblical view asserts that man is a creature totally dependent upon the Creator. He does not have parts, one of which automatically lives forever. Out of dust we were made, and to dust we return. In this respect, the biblical view is closer to that of the scientist than it is to the romantics who believe that they have an immortal soul.

The biblical view of man describes human life as wholly an act of God. Apart from God, man is not man, and dies. There is, in the biblical view, no answer to the question of who man is apart from his relationship to God. This is all said clearly by the German theologian Rudolf Bultmann:

> The demand for faith, therefore, is the demand that the world surrender the understanding it has had of itself hitherto—that it let the whole structure of its security which it has erected in presumptuous independence of the Creator fall to ruins. . . . Faith is turning away from the world, the act of desecularization, the surrender of all seeming security and every pretense, the willingness to live by the strength of the invisible and uncontrollable. It means accepting completely different standards as to what is to be called death and what life. It means accepting the life that Jesus gives and is—a life that to the world's point of view cannot even be proved to exist.[*]

*Rudolf Bultmann, *The Theology of the New Testament* (New York: Scribner's, 1955), II, p. 75.

Fuel for the Fire

The New Testament is permeated with this understanding of the meaning of human life and death. Sometimes it is explicit, as in the following passage from Paul.

> And you he made alive, when you were dead through the trespasses and sins in which you once walked, following the course of this world. . . . Among these we all once lived in the passions of our flesh, following the desires of body and mind, and so we were by nature children of wrath, like the rest of mankind. But God, who is rich in mercy, out of the great love with which he loved us, even when we were dead through our trespasses, made us alive together with Christ (by grace you have been saved), and raised us up with him and made us sit with him in the heavenly places in Christ Jesus . . . (Ephesians 2:1-6).

This passage makes no sense at all in terms of our common definition of life and death. Paul reminds the Ephesians that they were once dead. This certainly was not true according to the ordinary use of the word. What Paul meant was that they had been dead because of their trespasses and sins. They were dead because they were separated from God, the source of life. They had sought to take meaning from the world, which cannot give it. Thus, in the biblical view, it is possible to be alive in a nonbiblical sense and, at the same time, dead in the biblical sense of life and death. (See also the Parable of the Prodigal Son.)

There are words in this passage which are confusing to the English-speaking reader, for we tend to divide man into soul, spirit, mind, body, and flesh.

> In the biblical view, soul means life, which is never understood apart from man's relationship of dependence upon God. It is not an independent part of man installed by God at birth. In many instances where soul appears in the New Testament, the word life, or the word self, can be substituted. (Luke 12:22;

13

Romans 11:3. In Romans 2:9, the Greek word for soul is simply translated "human being" in the Revised Standard Version.)

The word spirit indicates man's source in God's Spirit, and the word self can sometimes be used synonomously with spirit.

Mind indicates primarily man's capacity for self-awareness and self-willing.

Body refers to the whole man, under his own control, freely governed by God, or under the sway of alien powers.

Flesh connotes man's identification with the rest of creation.

To understand the biblical view of man it is necessary to understand the biblical use of these words, as distinguished from the way in which they are used in our common language. We tend to see them purely as divisions of man and to think of them as unrelated to God. In the Bible, however, these words indicate relationships which man has to God, to other human beings, and to the balance of creation. They describe man as having self-awareness as a gift of God, as being created to live in a relationship with God. This is the biblical definition of life.

When the Bible describes all men as living in sin (alienation from God) and death (the consequence of sin), it does not mean that it is the material stuff of the earth, or our material bodies, which have been the cause of our death. It means that we have concentrated on ourselves, on other men, and on the "things of this world" to the exclusion of God. The guilt does not rest with what we have concentrated on, but with us for attaching too much importance to it. It is when men seek life this way that they live in death. (See Romans 6:15-23.)

Life, Death, and Jesus Christ

The gospel centers in the resurrection of Jesus Christ from the dead. He who was not dead in the biblical sense was made to know death, and from this death God raised him again to life. We are baptized into this death and into the promise of resurrection to life. This is Paul's witness in Romans 6:3-4:

14

"Do you not know that all of us who have been baptized into Christ Jesus were baptized into his death? We were buried therefore with him by baptism into death, so that as Christ was raised from the dead by the glory of the Father, we too might walk in newness of life."

There are many passages in John's Gospel which say this with equal directness. "Jesus said to him, 'I am the way, the truth, and the life . . .' " (John 14:6). "Jesus said to them, 'I am the bread of life; he who comes to me shall not hunger, and he who believes in me shall never thirst' " (John 10:10).

Since the biblical meaning of life and death makes sense only as disclosed to the eyes of faith and is a meaning which cannot be proved (by a scientific method), it is clear that it makes little sense apart from the biblical context to say that Jesus Christ is life, or gives life. The biblical view sees what we call natural death as the wages of sin. It also uses the word death to describe all living (in the natural sense) which is apart from God. Life is a word which has meaning, in biblical language, only for men who take their life from God. It is Christian teaching that no man by himself has life; rather, he takes his life from God. Nor does man have power in himself to turn from death to life. The focal witness of the gospel, therefore, is that God has raised Jesus Christ from the dead and restored him to life, and that this life he graciously grants to men who will receive it.

References and Resources

Kantonen, T. A. *Life After Death*. Philadelphia: Muhlenberg Press (Fortress Book), 1962.

Wilder, Thornton. *Our Town*, in *Three Plays*. New York: Harper, 1957.

See also:

John 11:25; Psalm 30:2-3; John 5:21, 24; Colossians 3:3-4; Colossians 2:13-15; Deuteronomy 30:19-20.

The *Small Catechism:* The Second Article of the Creed and the second section of The Sacrament of Holy Baptism.

the holy trinity 2

A series of questions concerning basic Christian doctrines was formulated by Dorothy Sayers and printed together with the kinds of answers which she felt the typical Christian would give. To the question "What is the doctrine of the Trinity?" the answer is "The Father incomprehensible, the Son incomprehensible, the whole thing incomprehensible. Something put in by theologians to make it more difficult—nothing to do with daily life or ethics."[*]

The best efforts of pastors, theologians, evangelists, and teachers have done little to improve the typical answer over the past decade. If anything, an increasing number of young adults reared in the age of scientific logic are offended by a doctrine which seems to make one sound like three, or three sound like one.

[*]Dorothy Sayers, *Creed or Chaos?* (New York: Harcourt, Brace, 1949), p. 22.

It is small comfort, but nevertheless true that the doctrine of the Trinity has been a major problem for every serious theologian. It is not that most theologians wish to deny the doctrine, or that they have questions concerning the truth which the doctrine seeks to convey. But they have found it difficult to communicate.

Sometimes we must smile at our efforts to put the majesty of almighty God into words. Nevertheless, the doctrine of the Trinity is basic to worship, teaching, and witness. It is essential to a faithful account of our knowledge of God. What follows cannot be a complete exposition of the doctrine, but it can indicate lines of further thought and investigation, and it can indicate some of the misconceptions which have proved barriers to concerned Christians.

One God

The beginning point is the simple confession that there is only one God. There are many things of which men make gods, and there are men who say that there are no gods at all, but Christians confess that there is only one God. This statement has no qualifications whatsoever concerning the number. We speak of the Father, and of the Son, and of the Holy Spirit, but he is one God. Some early Christians such as the Manichaeans taught that there were two gods: one of the Old Testament and one of the New Testament. But the Manichaeans were declared to be heretics because they had denied a basic confession of the church—namely, that there is only one God.

This basic confession is clearly affirmed in the first article of the *Augsburg Confession*.

> We unanimously hold and teach, in accordance with the decree of the Council of Nicaea, that there is one divine essence, which is called and which is truly God, and that there are three persons in this divine essence, equal in power and alike eternal: God the Father, God the Son, God the Holy Spirit. All three are one divine essence, eternal,

17

without division, without end, of infinite power, wisdom, and goodness, one creator and preserver of all things visible and invisible. . . .

One God, Revealed

In answer to a question by Thomas, Jesus is reported to have said, "I am the way, the truth, and the life; no one comes to the Father, but by me" (John 14:6). Whether or not John's Gospel is intended as a literal historical recording or is a doctrinally oriented witness of the early church makes little difference in our use and understanding of this passage. It affirms nothing more than is confessed in the whole New Testament and has been confessed by the church from that day to this: that no one is restored to God except through Christ. (Please note that "Christ" means more than the historical Jesus of 4-7 B.C.—c. A.D. 28. It means the eternal Word of God.)

This witness has been called everything from foolishness to nonsensical bigotry. It is so exclusive, so seemingly narrow-minded and outlandish, that no one in his right mind could accept it. The New Testament admits this. Martin Luther admitted it. In fact, it is sound Christian teaching to admit that restoration through Christ alone is unbelievable. Paul says this in 1 Corinthians 12:3: "Therefore I want you to understand that no one speaking by the Spirit of God ever says 'Jesus be cursed!' and no one can say 'Jesus is Lord' except by the Holy Spirit." In 1 Corinthians 2:12-13 he writes: "Now we have received not the spirit of the world, but the Spirit which is from God, that we might understand the gifts bestowed on us by God. And we impart this in words not taught by human wisdom, but taught by the Spirit, interpreting spiritual truths to those who possess the Spirit."

In Luther's explanation of the Third Article of the Creed in the *Small Catechism,* his words are, in one sense at least, a comfort to modern minds: "I believe that by my own reason or strength I cannot believe in Jesus Christ, my Lord, or come to him. But the Holy Spirit has called me through the Gospel, and enlightened me with his gifts. . . ."

18

Obviously, the earlier statement that the revelation of God in Christ is not believable now needs to be corrected. It is not believable in the sense that by ourselves we can hear the argument or the witness, ask our questions, and decide that it is true. If we confess its truth, it is because the Holy Spirit has called forth this response in us. Notice that this, too, is a witness of faith, not a purely rational statement which one could expect the non-Christian reader to accept as logically demonstrated. The Christian witness is that we are restored to God only in Jesus Christ, and that this knowledge is the gift of the Holy Spirit.

This is the point in the argument when logical people become indignant, for they see a position stated which is not only self-consistent, but also self-contained. Jesus Christ is the way, the truth, and the life. But the truth of this is known by the man of faith, not apart from faith. And faith is the gift of the Holy Spirit at work through the making of this witness, not through rational deductions.

The first response to this indignation is to affirm the first part — that Christian theology is self-consistent. The rational man has a right to demand this, and Christian teaching must demonstrate it. The second charge, that Christian teaching is self-contained, is also essentially to be affirmed. This teaching declares itself to be God's disclosure of himself, not man's discovery of God. It declares that our knowledge of him has been wholly his work, and not our own. This raises some questions about our role or participation in coming to faith, and these are discussed in the chapter on faith.

Revealer, Revelation, Revealedness

It is within this self-consistent understanding of revelation that the threefoldness of God permeates the New Testament and becomes central to Christian witness, teaching, and worship. We know the Father as revealer, the one God who has disclosed himself to men. We know the Father, the revealer, in his revelation, the Lord Jesus Christ. We know the Father

19

in Jesus Christ and this knowing is the fruit of the Spirit.

None of these three of God's ways of being God can exist separately. To be a revealer, one must provide a revelation. God is a revealer and his revelation is Jesus Christ (the only Son of the Father, the Word which was God). This has been revealed to us by the Holy Spirit. There must also be awareness of the revelation or the revealer. Without this, the revelation can have no significance.

As Claude Welch has stated:

> He makes himself known as the One who stands above and apart, the One to whom Jesus points as his Father and therefore our Father. At the same time, he is the One who confronts man in Jesus Christ as the objective content of revelation, i.e. the Son. And he is the One who seizes and possesses man so that he is able to receive and participate in revelation, new life, salvation, viz. the Holy Spirit.*

Many of us have been taught to think of the Holy Trinity as God at work in three different ways. He is the Creator, the Redeemer (in Jesus Christ), and the Sanctifier (in the work of the Holy Spirit). It cannot be said that such a definition is wrong, but it could be misleading. It sounds like a multiple job description, a simple spelling out of all that God has done. And this would not be the full teaching of the doctrine of the Trinity. We confess that God has not only *done* these things, but that he *is* triune. In contrast to the use of three verbs, we use three names, Father, Son, and Holy Spirit. The terms revealer, revelation, and revealedness are also nouns, used to describe God as he exists, not as verbs to describe what he does. God is revealer, revelation, and revealedness, and there was never a time when there was not this threefoldness in him. It is this inherent threefoldness in the very essence of God which allows Paul to say of Christ:

> He is the image of the invisible God, the first-born of all creation; for in him all things were created, in heaven and on earth, visible and invisible, whether thrones or dominions or

*Claude Welch, *In This Name* (New York: Scribner's, 1952), p. 282.

principalities, or authorities – all things were created through him and for him. He is before all things, and in him all things hold together.... For in him all the fulness of God was pleased to dwell... (Colossians 1:15-19).

If the Trinity is understood only in terms of the three major functions of God, it would not be possible for Paul to speak of Christ (redemption) as being from the beginning, and participating in creation. But the doctrine of the Trinity is more than a description of the three kinds of work which God has done or is doing. It is a description of God, who in his eternal essence is known to us as Father, Son, and Holy Spirit; as revealer, revelation, and revealedness.

Some Problems

In the first article of the *Augsburg Confession* and in our hymns and liturgies, there appears the word persons. The Confession says, "... And that there are three persons in this one divine essence...." Many theologians agree that this word is now a serious barrier. In the time of the church fathers and the Reformation, the Latin word *persona* was relatively ambiguous and was not defined as a separate and distinct center of responsibility. The modern meaning of the word is an inaccurate translation, however, implying three separate and distinct centers of responsibility, three separate divinities. The modern man who uses the term "God in three persons" must think of it as meaning something like "God in his threefoldness."

At the same time that we seek to avoid believing in three gods, we must not go to another extreme and allow the Son and the Holy Spirit to be swallowed up, so to speak, in the Godhead. God's revelation of himself as threefold means more than saying God has three functions. It means that God comes to us as a threefold divine being, and that, seen from the human side, there are ineradicable distinctions within the threefold nature of his being. For example, it is the Father who begets the Son, the Son (alone) who is incarnate and who

21

suffers and dies for mankind, and the Spirit who proceeds from the Father and the Son and grants faith, raises the dead, and bears ongoing witness to the mighty acts of God.

It is sometimes charged that the Trinity is a doctrine made by man, and that it is not essential to Christian teaching. It must be granted that it is man's formulation, as is true of every other doctrine. The question, however, is whether it arises of necessity out of the witness of the Scriptures and of the church. Do we find three gods in the Scriptures? Anyone at all acquainted with the Bible knows that the overwhelming witness is to one God. But it is equally true that the New Testament cannot be seriously read without encountering a threefoldness in what God discloses himself to be. Passages such as the one quoted from Colossians must either be ignored or taken seriously, and when taken seriously they lead inevitably toward the effort to provide an appropriate expression of the fullness of the God known through the Holy Spirit to be revealed in Jesus Christ. And so we say and sing "Glory be to the Father, and to the Son, and to the Holy Ghost; as it was in the beginning, is now, and ever shall be, one God, world without end."

References and Resources

Welch, Claude. *In This Name*. New York: Scribner's, 1952.
> *This is an excellent and helpful book, and the writer acknowledges his indebtedness. Welch is himself indebted to Karl Barth.*

See also:
Romans 8:27; John 1:1-13; John 16:7-15; Matthew 3:16-17; Matthew 12:25-32; Romans 8:14-16.

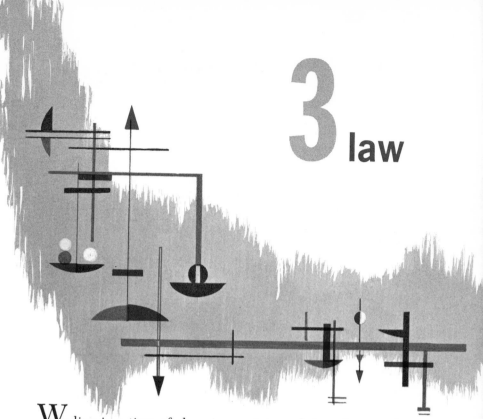

3 law

We live in a time of changing society and changing social values, and a number of books have been written in an attempt to analyze these changes and to prescribe for them. In one of these, the following passage appears.

> Numerous other value changes are appearing on the horizon as the mobile society seeks its answers. Religions, for example, are discovering that they must allow flexibility in their teachings to accommodate the changing society's needs. Intelligent clergymen of all faiths, particularly younger men, are seeing that it is more useful to encourage service to society than to require strict, letter-for-letter adherence to dogma and ritual. It may become necessary to teach old dogma new tricks.* '

*Richard Gordon, Katherine Gordon, and Max Gunther, *The Split-Level Trap* (New York: Geis, 1961), p. 309.

This is a bad joke, but the authors of *The Split-Level Trap* can be forgiven that. The passage is instructive, representing as it probably does the sentiment of a large number of thoughtful people. A number of assumptions are made. To say that the church "must allow flexibility in [its] teachings" assumes that such flexibility is presently lacking. "To accommodate the changing society's needs" implies that the function of church teaching is to serve the needs of society, whatever they may be. The term "useful" indicates something of the same approach. Again, the passage assumes that service to the community and adherence to dogma and ritual are antithetical. Finally, there is the hint of a suggestion that "intelligent" church leaders can train dogma to do what they think should be done.

Most of these assumptions are based upon a particular understanding of the nature of law in Christian teaching. What, in Christian terminology, is "the law"? How do we distinguish among natural law, civil law, ecclesiastical law, and the law of Christ? How rigid and fixed is the law? What is the relationship between the law and the gospel? After we have considered these questions, we may be in a better position to know whether "intelligent clergymen" will be able to make God's law do "new tricks" to meet "society's needs."

The Law of God and Civil Law

Most countries have a law which says that you must drive on a particular side of the road, except on one-way streets and under other specific circumstances. This is a civil law. It was made by men in order to establish some order on streets and highways. It was not necessary in the promotion of such a law for the legislators to make any reference to God or the Bible. The law can be changed to require that everyone drive on the other side. It's possible, but not likely, for it to be rescinded altogether.

The roots of such a law are probably pragmatic. It's more efficient and safer if we adhere to a common practice on the highway. Even those who voted for the law because it meant fewer injuries and deaths need have no use for God and the Fifth Commandment. They could have been genuinely interested in man's welfare, concerned for lost man-hours in the economy, or anxious about their personal safety.

There is a common tradition among most men that there are certain rights which belong inherently to every human being and which are inalienable. These rights are sometimes said to be rooted in "the natural law." They spring out of the order of things; they are known to all right-minded men; they have universal validity; they judge all civil laws and ordinances. Various efforts have been made to identify these inherent rights. The Constitution of the United States includes a Bill of Rights; the Commission of Human Rights of the United Nations has made a fuller statement; the Atlantic Charter sought to identify man's rightful freedoms.

Among these inherent rights is the right to live. Under certain circumstances, in some countries, this right can be taken away or placed in jeopardy (wartime military service, for example), but this is considered a necessary infringement of a basic right. Uncontrolled use of the highway is a threat to the right to live, so it could be said that a law restricting this use is rooted in a basic human right.

There is, therefore, a happy agreement between a civil law which seeks to preserve the right to live and a commandment of God which forbids killing or bids us love our neighbor. These two meet at the point where the man of God confesses that God has implanted the desire to live in the very structures of creation and that most men, whether they confess God or not, have found it there and cherish it. To the man of God, these basic human rights and the laws which arise to protect them are a part of God's law, established in creation. Others may call them inherent, inalienable, and natural.

Beyond the law of creation (or the natural law) which most men honor, we speak of the laws or the commands of God as they are revealed in the Old and New Testaments. We confess that these commandments are also binding upon all men, but

25

the knowledge that this is true is the knowledge which faith gives.

The authors of *The Split-Level Trap* feel that some mature individuals should not be discouraged from extramarital sex relationships. You see, they find no justification for exclusion of such behavior in the natural law. Their suggested change in the value system is based upon what they assume will be useful in suburban society. Their suggestion, however, that the church support this change in morals assumes both that the church agrees that such freedom is not against the natural law and that their criterion (usefulness) would be approved by the church. The church, however, is to be obedient to the revealed law of God as well as natural law. We must not ask "Would it be useful?" but "Is it in accordance with the will of God as revealed in the Old and New Testaments?"

We could argue with the authors that such a change in the value structure would not, in fact, be useful. They would have to take this argument seriously, since it is based on their own criterion of usefulness. We could also make the witness which grows out of God's revelation. But unless they were also called through faith to obedience, they would not be likely to agree to our position.

It is impossible to separate clearly the law of God as it is known to the natural man in creation and the law of God as revealed in the Scriptures. It is possible, in a general way, to distinguish them. Most civil law is rooted ultimately in an effort to provide the kind of order which the world itself requires and which can be called the law of creation or, by others, the natural law. God's revealed law is binding upon all men, but it can be known only through the knowledge which faith gives.

The Form and Content of the Law

The revelation of God in the Old Testament comes through his struggle with his people Israel. The two themes which inform the whole are God's act of love in the deliverance of

Israel out of Egypt, and the giving of the Law through which the covenant relationship was to be sustained. Moses' speech to the people in the eight chapter of Deuteronomy is characteristic of this relationship of grace and law, showing what God does for his people and what he requires of them.

> "For the LORD your God is bringing you into a good land.... And you shall eat and be full, and you shall bless the LORD your God for the good land he has given you. Take heed lest you forget the LORD your God, by not keeping his commandments and his ordinances and his statutes, which I command you this day...."

In the beginning was the garden, provided by a gracious God. But in the beginning also was the command not to eat of a particular tree. The man is blessed whose delight is in the law of the Lord; and he who is not blessed is like chaff. "The Lord knows the way of the righteous, but the way of the wicked will perish" (Psalm 1:6).

God made a covenant with his people (Exodus 24). This was wholly God's act and by it he made them his own. But the structure of the relationship was the Law. His own were to hear his words and do them. And the response of the people to the covenant of God was "All that the LORD has spoken we will do, and we will be obedient" (Exodus 24:7).

The great storms and the quiet laments of the Old Testament tell another story. The people worshiped other gods; their response to God was stale and dead; they neglected the times of praise and thanksgiving which nourish life in the Creator. His people killed, committed adultery, were thieves and liars and covetous men (Exodus 20). They could not do these things and be God's people. He would hold a plumbline against their crookedness and judge them worthy of death (Amos 7:7). His commandments would be the measure of their death (Deuteronomy 30:19; Jeremiah 21:8). The Lord had a great controversy with his people (Micah 6:2). The prophecy of Hosea is a beautiful and powerful witness to God's compassion for a people who must nevertheless be judged unfaithful and alienated from life.

27

The despair of men who honor the law but cannot fulfill its demands, is spoken by Paul:

> So I find it to be a law that when I want to do right, evil lies close at hand. For I delight in the law of God, in my inmost self, but I see in my members another law at war with the law of my mind and making me captive to the law of sin which dwells in my members. Wretched man that I am! Who will deliver me from this body of death? (Romans 7:21-23).

The despair which resulted from the failure to keep the law was, in one basic sense, intensified by the teaching of Jesus Christ. The formal keeping of the law was not enough. It was not a question of what one did, but a question of motivations, of the orientation of the heart in which the actions were rooted. It was not to be the question of whether one killed or refrained from killing, but a question of whether one loved his brother (Matthew 5:27). It could no longer be considered adequate to refrain from adultery. Man would be measured by the meaning of a look in his eye (Matthew 5:28).

The law in the teaching of Christ is elevated to love, a spontaneous life centered in the praise of God and joyful self-forgetfulness in service to other men.

Love is, on the one hand, the fulfillment of the law of the Old Testament. It encompasses all of the intentions of the old covenant, sharpens and heightens them, and moves beyond. This means, on the other hand, that the old law is in fact outmoded. It cannot, with its patterned and formal legalisms, contain the spontaneous life lived in love. It is an old wineskin which is inadequate for the new wine (Matthew 9:17).

The Law, the Gospel, and Life in the World

The Christian faith confesses that while man is still caught and held by sin and alienated from God, this same God has bridged this gulf in Jesus Christ and restores man unto himself (Romans 5). It is, therefore, *sinful* man who is restored to life through God's grace (Ephesians 2:4ff.) Two things become clear to the Christian man. He knows that he is called to live in

28

joy and freedom because he has been restored to the source and meaning of life by God himself and the judgment of the law cannot terrify his conscience. At the same time, he knows that so long as he lives in the world he will continue to sin, and the law does judge his life. The Christian man therefore lives by "daily repentance and Baptism," seeks to grow in love, and lives in the expectation of the act of God by which the warfare will be ended.

The Christian, therefore, knows a love which has freely and without merit on his part sought him out. He knows that he is to rejoice in this freedom, and to live a life of spontaneous love for his neighbor. As an individual, this will motivate him to seek ways of traveling on the highway in order that he may protect the life of his neighbor. It may also motivate him to respect the vow of faithfulness which marriage announces and to shun acts which would violate such vows. He is constrained by the love of Christ. The usefulness of another value system cannot be his criterion.

Yet the Christian also knows that he continues to sin, and that he lives in a sinful world. He therefore seeks, with other men, the establishment of laws which are rooted in the law of creation and which all men may agree are "inherent in the natural order."

When the Christian man, therefore, seeks to legislate order on the highway, he may be motivated by love for his neighbor. He argues his case, however, on the basis of the law of creation—that men have a right to life, and such and such a law will serve that end.

When the Christian man hears the suggestion that it would be useful to society to change the value structure to allow extramarital sex relationships, he may disagree on the basis that he cannot do this and fulfill the law of Christ. But in the world he must argue that such a value change would violate the justice required by the natural law, or that it would not, in fact, be useful in the community.

There is a civil law, which serves the cause of order among sinful men. The Christian is called to honor it.

There is the law of God revealed in the Old Testament. The Christian acknowledges that under this law he would be condemned to alienation from God, the source of life.

There is the way of Christ, rooted in God's forgiveness of sinners in his Son, which sets us free for spontaneous and unselfish service to our neighbor. We live with the sounds of this in our hearts, seeking to live it now, and hoping for perfection in a time — or beyond time — when God's will is completely followed from the hearts of men.

References and Resources

Aulén, Gustaf. *The Faith of the Christian Church*. Philadelphia: Muhlenberg Press, 1948.
> *See especially pages 37-47.*
Niebuhr, H. Richard. *Christ and Culture*. New York: Harper, 1951.
> *See especially pages 170-189.*

See also:
The *Small Catechism*, The Ten Commandments. *The heightening and sharpening of the Old Testament law is clearly reflected in Luther's explanations of these Commandments.*
The *Augsburg Confession. Articles XX and XXVII both illustrate the freedom from the law which is granted in Jesus Christ. It will be helpful to read them in the light of this chapter. See also Articles XVI and XXVIII on the role of civil law.*

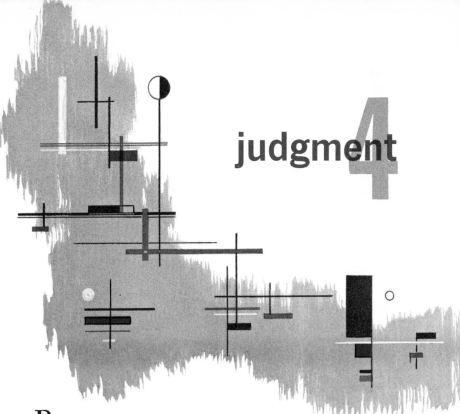

judgment4

Brother Juniper, in Thornton Wilder's novel *The Bridge of San Luis Rey,* knew that all evil was God's punishment designed to improve our lives, and that all good was God's reward. He needed only the right circumstance to prove this to men slow of heart to believe. When the bridge of San Luis Rey collapsed after more than a century of service it carried five people to their deaths. Brother Juniper spent six years collecting the evidence which would allow him to prove that good men had been brought quickly to heaven, and evil men had received their just reward.

These incidents provided Wilder an opportunity to make his own point. Regardless of what Brother Juniper said, the life of each of the five was compounded of good and evil, and it made no sense to call the collapse of the bridge a punishment for some and a reward for others. In fact, the true circumstances made a travesty of Brother Juniper's concept of God's justice and providence.

In the thirteenth chapter of Luke's Gospel a similar incident is reported:

> There were some present at that very time who told him of the Galileans whose blood Pilate had mingled with their sacrifices. And he answered them, "Do you think that these Galileans were worse sinners than all other Galileans, because they suffered thus? I tell you, No; but unless you repent, you will all likewise perish" (Luke 13:1-3).

The Galileans were at worship when Pilate killed them. Were they punished by God because of the extreme nature of their sins? The answer given by our Lord is "No." Thornton Wilder was right, Job was right, and so also are a host of less literate men who cannot agree with those who say that every act of suffering is imposed by God for specific sins. This is one part of Christian teaching concerning judgment: we are not to see every tragic event as the direct judgment of God upon those struck down.

The concluding sentence of Christ's answer, however, is equally instructive: "... But unless you repent, you will all likewise perish." There is a judgment of God which falls upon sinful men. Our task, then, is to understand this aspect of God's self-disclosure, to relate it to the love which we know in Christ, and to see what relevance this judgment has on our lives.

Life Under Judgment

Although some deny every aspect of human freedom, consigning us to the role of robots conditioned by heredity and culture, most observers of man consider that man possesses a measure of individual freedom by which to make a few choices which he may call his own. As judged by the civil law, most people can be called good and law-abiding citizens. The Christian is not so alienated from the world that he can't use the terms good man, sweet child, gracious lady, and fine person. And when we use these terms, we mean to imply that these virtues actually belong to the person. They describe the way in which the person has used his freedom.

But notice that these judgments are usually made on the basis of the civil code or the standards of the culture. The Christian who has said with full integrity that someone is a good man can say with equal integrity that this same man is a sinner who lives under the judgment of God. There is really no confusion here, unless we confuse the standards by which goodness is measured. The same men and women who are judged by their fellowmen to be saintly in comparison with other men confess themselves to be sinners before God.

We are all judged sinners, regardless of our civil goodness. We were created free. This is the major point of the story of Adam and Eve in the Garden of Eden. They were free to eat the apple or to be obedient, for example. The difference between Adam and Eve and all who have followed them is that we are not completely free to be obedient. We are not free to accept another person as he is, or to give friendship or love without obligations. We really can't help ourselves, and it is not a matter of a lack of courage or will power. It is now a matter of our basic nature.

Therefore, the Christian speaks easily about civil goodness, easily names the virtues of his contemporaries, and easily speaks of man's freedom to make basic decisions. At the same time, the Christian places his life before the mirror which God holds, and confesses that he does not love as God loves him, and that he is not even free to choose to love as God loves him. He confesses also that this places him under the judgment of God because he cannot live a truly righteous life.

Already Condemned

The basic dynamic of God's judgment is expressed in the following passage from John's Gospel.

> For God so loved the world that he gave his only Son, that whoever believes in him should not perish but have eternal

33

life. For God sent the Son into the world, not to condemn the world, but that the world might be saved through him. He who believes in him is not condemned; he who does not believe is condemned already, because he has not believed in the name of the only Son of God. And this is the judgment, that the light has come into the world, and men loved darkness rather than light, because their deeds were evil (John 3:16-19).

The condition of man to which these words are addressed is the condition of sin and death. Christ came to save man from this. Christ did not come to condemn the world. Men were already condemned. The question is whether or not men will accept the forgiveness revealed in Christ—will they accept this way, this truth, this life, which is Christ? If not, they are already judged and there is no help. Will they accept the proffered forgiveness? If not, they continue to perish and to live under judgment.

Judgment in this respect is not a special act of God, but a state which is implicit in man's creation. The source of life is in God. The man who will not take his life from God lives in death. There is no need for God to make some kind of judicial decision, saying "How has this fellow done? Is he good or bad?" The question is "Where is his life rooted? What nourishes him?" If the answer is "He feeds upon himself and his fellowmen," that's all that needs to be said. Such nourishment comes from a poisoned well, and the judgment is more like an announcement—we are already condemned.

The Wrath and Love of God

So great has been the sense of God's judgment upon their lives that men like the second-century Christian Marcion postulated both an Old Testament God of wrath, and a New Testament God of love. Though this was a radical solution of the problem and was declared heretical, Christians have often tended to swing like a pendulum, stressing first one and then the other.

34

Christian teaching knows no such division. God is love, and all that we may call wrath, anger, judgment, and condemnation actually grow out of the love of God. A parent loves a child and because this is so he insists that the child not go into the street. This same love will be the source of his punishment if he disobeys.

Obviously, however, the parent does not get out his car and run down his child in order to punish him. On the other hand, if a car does hit a child who runs into the street, both the parents and the child understand that disobedience has indeed been "punished" or, better, has had its effect.

This is a valid distinction when we talk about the wrath of God. Brother Juniper wanted to say that God caused the Bridge of San Luis Rey to collapse. This was based upon a mistaken understanding of God's relationship to the world. It is not necessary for the parent to hit his child with a car. It is not necessary for God to collapse a bridge. There is enough evil in the world without adding to it. The child may learn from being hit, and a population may learn from the collapse of a bridge, and Christian people may say, "God has punished and instructed us." But there is a vast difference between confessing that some good has come of evil and saying that God caused the evil in the first place.

God's wrath and judgment, then, are to be seen as inherent parts of his love. If love meant indulgence, the loved ones would be allowed to gorge themselves to death without the protest of the lover. This could not be called love.

Moreover, this must be seen in its social context. When men seek to take their lives by feeding upon their neighbors, they face the angry love of God, concerned not only for their salvation but also for the life and dignity of the neighbor, whom he also loves.

Final Judgment

There is a tendency to speak of the final judgment in terms of the Old Testament law. To what extent have we kept the law? This will be the measure by which we ascend to heaven or descend into hell. This concept is also present in the New Testament:

> Do not marvel at this; for the hour is coming when all who are in the tombs will hear his voice and come forth, those who have done good, to the resurrection of life, and those who have done evil, to the resurrection of judgment (John 5:28-29).

However, the basic New Testament concept is that the final judgment will determine, not whether we have kept the law, but whether we come trusting in the forgiveness of God made known in Jesus Christ. Such faith will have borne the fruits of good works, of course. It is important to note that both the *Augsburg Confession* (Article III) and the *Catechism* (Third article of the Creed) emphasize the biblical teaching (Acts 10:42) that Christ is our judge.

So we meet in the Scriptures a concept of a present judgment which describes the condition of all who live outside the love of God. And the source of this judgment is the love of God. We also have the witness of a judgment which is to come, when the dead are raised. But it is difficult to know why those who have lived in alienation from God and died in alienation from God should be raised from the dead. Perhaps it is precisely in order that they may see clearly that they are in fact dead, and will remain so. And perhaps this seeing clearly is the meaning of hell. But if seeing clearly, they then repent...?

References and Resources

Aulén, Gustaf. *The Faith of the Christian Church,* pp. 138-153.
Heinecken, Martin J. *Basic Christian Teachings.* Philadelphia: Muhlenberg Press, 1949, pp. 52-58, 129-138.
Wilder, Thornton. *The Bridge of San Luis Rey.* New York: Albert and Charles Boni, 1927.

See also:
Revelation 16:1-7; Isaiah 30:30; Isaiah 33:22; Romans 14:10-12; 1 Corinthians 15.

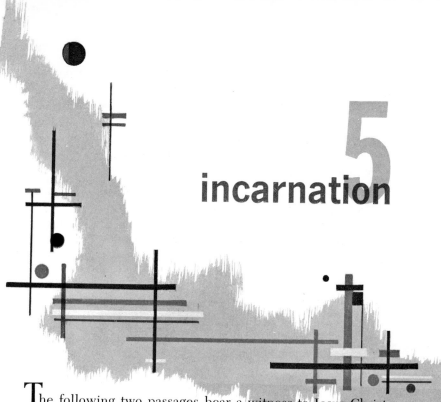

incarnation 5

The following two passages bear a witness to Jesus Christ which is present in the whole of the New Testament—the witness that God came among men in Jesus Christ to reconcile the world unto himself:

> For the law was given through Moses; grace and truth came through Jesus Christ. No one has ever seen God; the only Son, who is in the bosom of the Father, he has made him known (John 1:17-18).

> He is the image of the invisible God, the first-born of all creation. . . . He is before all things, and in him all things hold together. . . . For in him all the fullness of God was pleased to dwell, and through him to reconcile to himself all things, whether on earth or in heaven, making peace by the blood of his cross (Colossians 1:15-20).

From the very beginning, this witness was strange and incomprehensible to many, and there was need to state it with as much precision as the language of the time and the character of the event allowed. In the earliest church, the convert confessed his faith with simplicity, saying merely "Jesus Christ is Lord." In time, the baptismal confession was added to until it became the Apostle's Creed. At the Council of Nicea in A.D. 325, the church summarized the witness of the Scriptures in the following words:

> And in one Lord Jesus Christ, the only-begotten Son of God, Begotten of his Father before all worlds, God of God, Light of Light, Very God of very God, Begotten, not made, Being of one substance with the Father, By whom all things were made: Who for us men, and for our salvation, came down from heaven, And was incarnate by the Holy Ghost of the Virgin Mary, And was made man; and was crucified also for us under Pontius Pilate. . . .

Even our great familiarity with such passages from the creeds of the church cannot blunt the striking assertion which they make. Battles have been fought and Western civilization shaken to the core in efforts to preserve at full strength all that is implied in these creeds. Great treasure and thousands of lives have been spent in carrying this witness concerning Christ into every part of the world. Literally tons of books have been written to interpret it and to call the people of Christ to praise and adoration. The greatest music and art of our Western culture have been measures of man's response.

But none of this can take the place of our own effort to understand what the church has meant by the witness that God became incarnate in Jesus Christ.

The Incarnation as Event

The word time has different meanings. Time may pass quickly or slowly; it also passes with measured precision. It is high time, or about time, or some time. And all of these personal and impersonal ways of considering time have now been further modified by modern physics, which measures time in relation to such things as the speed of light and the

38

mass of an object and relative positions in a space-time continuum.

When the church speaks of God becoming incarnate in Jesus Christ it means that this was an event occurring visibly in the midst of the ordered progression of days and years. According to Luke, it occurred in the days of Herod the king, in the time of the Emperor Augustus, when P. Sulpicius Quirinius was governor of Syria.

God's coming in the time of Herod is an incarnation which we describe in our clock-approach to time. From God's point of view, superior to our ideas of time, the Christ "always" existed and "always" will, "world without end."

It should not be assumed that because God came into time it can be proved that it was indeed he who was in Christ. Some men will argue that nothing which happens in history can be proved in any absolute way. But to whatever extent it can be proved, the historian as historian knows only that there was a man named Jesus of Nazareth who left his mark upon some of the people of Palestine nearly two thousand years ago. The confession that God was revealing himself in Christ is known only by faith. This is the knowledge called forth by God himself.

True Man and True God

The New Testament is a witness or proclamation and not a textbook of doctrine. In the words of Paul, "He is the image of the invisible God, the first-born of all creation..." (Colossians 1:15). Men of faith hear this and rejoice. But it is necessary that the man of faith face the questions which he is able to ask and which will be asked of him by others. What does image mean? Is he the image because he worked at it, or because God worked at it? Was Jesus a real person, or was he a filmy appearance of God?

The doctrines of the church have been forged in answer to such questions. They are never final and definitive statements and were never designed to take the place of proclamation, but they do serve both the teaching responsibility of the church and the defense of its witness.

In answer to the questions concerning Christ the church has affirmed the biblical witness that he was truly man. There was a man in Philadelphia (Pennsylvania) called Father Divine, and one of the marks of his divinity was that he reputedly never slept. Jesus made no such pretense. He slept. He had need of food. He died. A whole section of the Apostles' Creed is given to saying this: "Born of the Virgin Mary, Suffered under Pontius Pilate, Was crucified, dead and buried." Although the emphasis in the first phrase has tended to fall upon "Virgin," the obvious intention is to stress the fact that he was born, suffered, was crucified, died, and was buried. There is no equivocation. This Jesus of Nazareth was not an elusive spirit appearing temporarily in the guise of a man. Such a concept would have scandalized the Christians who gave us the words of the New Testament.

With equal vigor the church has asserted of Christ that "in him all the fullness of God was pleased to dwell. . ." (Colossians 1:19). One of the first questions asked concerning this is: Did Christ so understand himself? The question can be answered only in terms of the witness of the church. The words of Christ are the words remembered and set down by men of faith. Their witness is that he did so understand himself. Luke reports, for example, that Jesus went into the synagogue, read the prophecy of Isaiah concerning the Servant of the Lord, and said, "Today this scripture has been fulfilled in your hearing" (Luke 4:16-21). John makes this witness:

> Jesus answered them, "I told you, and you do not believe. The works that I do in my Father's name, they bear witness to me; but you do not believe, because you do not belong to my sheep. My sheep hear my voice, and I know them, and they follow me; and I give them eternal life, and they shall never perish, and no one shall snatch them out of my hand. My Father, who has given them to me, is greater than all, and no one is able to snatch them out of the Father's hand. I and the Father are one" (John 10:25-30).

40

The claim was the one which led eventually to his crucifixion—that he and the Father were one.

The witness that we encounter God in this Christ does not rest on the remembered words of Christ concerning himself. His followers gave this same testimony when they spoke of his miraculous birth, the authority with which he taught, the events of his death, and the impact of his resurrection. The witness that it was God who had come among them in Christ was the core of all their preaching, the very heart of their worship, and the reason for their mission.

We may protest that God should have made all of this indisputably clear. Instead, in the very act of revealing himself he remained hidden. He is hidden in a Nazarene carpenter, announced by preaching, and recognized only by those who do not refuse the enlightening guidance of his Spirit.

The Limitations of Reason

To say that Christ was truly man, and at the same time truly God, serves to protect the witness of the Scriptures, but it leaves unanswered the question of how this can be. Faith does not fully comprehend this, but some things can be said.

The first is that the greatest stumbling block to this confession is to imagine that the God and Christ are somehow physically the same. This is contrary both to the witness of faith and to common sense. To say, in the words of the Nicene Creed, that Father and Son are of the same "substance" is misleading if we assume that substance means something physical. The substance of God is his loving will. The confession of the creed is, therefore, that the love and will which we behold in Christ is the loving will of God.

This still leaves the problem of how we can consider Christ fully man if he doesn't "have his own will." In passage after passage, the Scriptures indicate dialogue between Father and Son (the prayer in the garden, for example).

The resolution of this problem may lie somewhere in the nature of love. Love has the capacity to win response without, in the process, detracting from the wholeness of the one loved.

41

The facts are, of course, that it is impossible for finite man to understand infinite God or how he could become finite. We see "as in a mirror, dimly."

Some Implications

The many implications of the Incarnation will be more fully developed in the chapters which follow. Two things are of immediate importance.

First, the Incarnation is a focal point for distinguishing Christianity in particular from religion in general. It announces that God has drawn near to reveal himself in distinction to man's effort to find himself or God through "religion." The Incarnation is God's own bridging of the distance between Creator and creation. It announces the visible presence of the invisible God, his coming from beyond the outer reaches to the roads where men walk. This is almost impossible to comprehend. But for the man with faith, the Incarnation is the foundation of Christian teaching.

The second implication of the Incarnation is a reaffirmation of the material stuff of the world. Man is a slave to sin, but God despises neither man nor the world but comes to redeem the whole. This is the root of the Christian's joy in material things, which contrasts so sharply with the negation of the world by countless pious people who do not know or understand that the Word became flesh and dwelt among us.

References and Resources

Aulén, Gustaf. *The Faith of the Christian Church,* pp. 210-222.
Brunner, Emil. *Revelation and Reason.* Philadelphia: Westminster, 1946. Chapter 15.
Heinecken, Martin J. *Basic Christian Teachings,* pp. 71-74.
Wolf, William J. *No Cross, No Crown.* New York: Doubleday, 1957.

See also:
Ephesians 3:7-13; John 1; Acts 9; Luke 22:39-46.
Small Catechism, Second Article of the Creed.
Augsburg Confession, Article III.

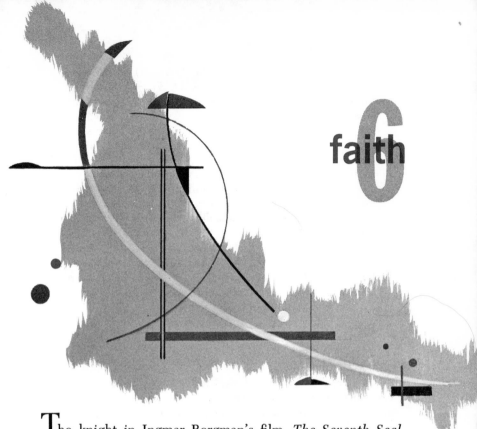

faith 6

The knight in Ingmar Bergman's film, *The Seventh Seal,* has returned from the Crusades. Filled with a sense of futility, he finds the countryside scourged by the plague. Death has come to him, but he has bargained for time to do one meaningful deed. On his homeward journey, he stops in a small chapel and goes to the grilled opening to make his confession.

> I want to talk to you as openly as I can, but my heart is empty. — The emptiness is a mirror turned toward my own face. I see myself in it, and I am filled with fear and disgust. Through my indifference to my fellow men, I have isolated myself from their company. Now I live in a world of phantoms, I am imprisoned in my dreams and fantasies.
> CONFESSOR: And yet you don't want to die.
> KNIGHT: Yes, I do.
> CONFESSOR: You want guarantees?

43

KNIGHT: Call it whatever you like. Is it so cruelly inconceivable to grasp God with the senses? Why should he hide himself in a mist of half-spoken promises and unseen miracles? How can we have faith in those who believe when we can't have faith in ourselves? What is going to happen to those of us who want to believe but aren't able to? And what is to become of those who neither want to nor are capable of believing? Why can't I kill God within me? Why does he live on in this painful and humiliating way even though I curse Him and want to tear Him out of my heart? Why, in spite of everything, is He a baffling reality that I can't shake off? Do you hear me?

CONFESSOR: Yes, I hear you.

KNIGHT: I want knowledge, not faith, not suppositions, but knowledge. I want God to stretch out his hand toward me, reveal Himself, and speak to me.*

This is an honest statement. It represents the kind of internal struggle undergone by large numbers of people who earnestly desire to know God and believe in him. But it also represents misunderstandings about the nature of faith. Bergman suggests this by showing the Confessor, listening to the knight from behind the grill, to be Death. The purpose of this chapter is to indicate what faith *does* mean in the language and teaching of the church.

To Know

Though we may sometimes pay homage to the idiosyncrasies of a car by giving her a name, "Betsy" eventually becomes an "it" again and is traded or sold for junk. We acknowledge a vast measure of identification between ourselves and the things of the world, but we also make a few distinctions. One of them is the difference in the way in which we know things, and the way in which we know people.

This is not to say that people can't be known in the same way that we know things. That's the way it is, or seems at least,

*Ingmar Bergman, *Four Screenplays* (New York: Simon and Schuster, 1960), pp. 111-112. By permission.

when we are inducted into the armed forces. We are known by height, weight, scars, teeth, and a number.

This is increasingly true in the civilian world, too. We are the people in the apartment over the drugstore, or locker number 607, or the man in the blue collar, white collar, or gray flannel. We have a ZIP-code number, a Social Security number, a bank-account number.

But we also may know one another in a different way. It may be called friendship; however, "knowing" means much more than that. Understanding is a part of it. But it comes closer to being a mutual self-disclosure of the inmost self, the self which can be known only as we allow this to happen. It's possible to *know* a person in this sense, and really know little *about* him.

Martin Buber, the Jewish theologian, has given us simple words with which to make these distinctions. "I-It" describes our relationship to things. "I-He" describes a relationship with a person, but the person is known objectively. "I-Thou" describes subjectively the profound encounter of two persons in which one man's knowledge of another has grown out of mutual self-disclosure.

Now, consider the plea of the knight in the film. He acknowledges that he has isolated himself from his fellowmen and feels a great emptiness. At the same time, he demands to know God with his senses and rebels against "half-spoken promises and unseen miracles." This is an impossible combination! How can the invisible God be known to the eyes? How can the God who is Spirit make sounds for the ear to hear, or stand forth for the hands to measure? Furthermore, even if this were possible, this would be the knowing described by "I-He," not the "I-Thou" knowledge which the word faith describes.

Neither does the knowledge which faith gives come to us in isolation from our fellowmen. The context in which God is known is precisely the context of human relationships – of mutual self-disclosure in love and hate, jealousy, and anger. To whatever extent the knight is granted faith, it comes to him through the love he finds in a strolling player, his wife, and his child. In response to what he beholds in them, the knight in Bergman's story yields to death in order that these three people may escape.

Evangelical Christians rarely use the term dogma because it carries the connotation of "that which must be believed." One can be related to dogma only as "It." It is important to know what the church teaches. But it must always be clear that we do not mean to equate Christian faith with the acceptance of certain teachings. Christian faith is the knowledge of God and trust in him which grows out of God's own self-disclosure, the relationship of I-Thou.

Emil Brunner writes, "Faith is therefore first of all an act of knowledge; it is the 'light of the knowledge of the glory of God,' it is awareness of the God who reveals Himself."*

Trust and Obedience

The knowledge of God which faith describes has at least two attributes: trust and obedience. Just as faith is not an act of decision, but is called forth by the God who discloses himself, so also trust and obedience are not personal decisions. One of the things we learn in the experience of faith is that God is trustworthy. We know this. Thus faith means a radical change in our orientation. Apart from God, our ultimate concern is for ourselves, our fellowmen, our nation, and so forth. The root of our anxiety is in our knowledge or feeling that we are trusting in someone or something which is finite, and therefore, in the end, untrustworthy. But faith provides the knowledge that God is always trustworthy, and thus he becomes the source of a new freedom and confidence. This is the root of all the joy of the New Testament. In Brunner's words:

> Confidence (or trust) is the heart of faith. This trust means the act by which we abandon ourselves without reserve into the hands of God. In this act of trust the deepest instinct of the human heart—and, where God is concerned, the worst

*Emil Brunner, *Revelation and Reason* (Philadelphia: Westminster, 1946), p. 34.

sin of man—is overcome: the instinct of self-preservation, the desire to "paddle one's own canoe."[*]

The knowledge of God which faith describes also calls forth obedience. We find him to be loving will, and obedience to his will becomes a responsive act of thanksgiving.

Faith and Doubt

All that has been said about the meaning of faith is summarized by Paul in the third chapter of his Epistle to the Philippians. The trust and obedience which reoriented his whole life is expressed first:

> But whatever gain I had, I counted as loss for the sake of Christ. Indeed I count everything as loss because of the surpassing worth of knowing Christ Jesus my Lord. For his sake I have suffered the loss of all things, and count them as refuse, in order that I may gain Christ and be found in him, not having a righteousness of my own, based on law, but that which is through faith in Christ, the righteousness from God that depends on faith... (Philippians 3:7-9).

In the verses which follow Paul says again that his faith—his knowledge of God, his trust and obedience—was not of his own doing.

> Not that I have already obtained this or am already perfect; but I press on to make it my own, because Christ Jesus has made me his own. Brethren, I do not consider that I have made it my own... (Philippians 3:12-13).

But there is also another suggestion in this passage. Paul has not appropriated, even to the extent possible in this life, the gifts of faith—knowledge, trust, obedience. God in Christ has reached out to Paul and made him his own. Therefore, Paul will press on to lay hold of gifts which he has not perfectly appropriated.

This is the sense in which the word doubt is used in Christian teaching. If faith were a matter of believing certain

[*]*Ibid.*, p. 35.

facts, doubt would war against such belief. But faith is described as a knowledge of God analogous to our knowledge of another person. Even at the human level, there is never a full appropriation of the depths of a man's person. In our relationship with God, we know him with a certainty, but at the same time must confess uncertainty before one who cannot be encircled and held captive by finite men.

This element of uncertainty in faith is expressed by Paul Tillich in the following way:

> An act of faith is an act of a finite being who is grasped by and turned to the infinite. It is a finite act with all the limitations of a finite act, and it is an act in which the infinite participates beyond the limitations of a finite act. Faith is certain in so far as it is an experience of the holy. But faith is uncertain in so far as the infinite to which it is related is received by a finite being. This element of uncertainty in faith cannot be removed, it must be accepted. And the element in faith which accepts this is courage.[*]

Faith and Life

Faith is a knowledge of God which God himself calls forth as we live among our fellowmen and hear the witness to his revelatory acts in Jesus Christ. In this calling forth of faith, God instills in us not only knowledge, but trust and obedience.

Even in our closest human relationships there are relatively few times when we fully sense the oneness expressed by "I-Thou." Husband and wife live together in loyalty to these experiences of oneness, and in anticipation of future experiences.

The Christian must not, therefore, assume that God will always be an overwhelming reality. Much of our life is spent in loyalty to the faith which this experience has nourished, and will nourish again.

[*]Paul Tillich, *The Dynamics of Faith* (New York: Harper Torchbooks, 1958), p. 16.

References and Resources

Tillich, Paul. *The Dynamics of Faith*. New York: Harper Torchbooks, 1958.

This is an excellent book for those who wish to pursue "the dynamics of faith" in a thorough way.

See also:

Small Catechism, Third Article of the Creed. *Reference has been made to Luther's explanation in an earlier chapter, but it should be read again at this point.*

Augsburg Confession, Article XX. *This is a key article and should receive careful attention. Both the concept of faith and the relationship of obedience (good works) are clearly stated.*

Ephesians 2:8-9; Romans 5:1. *Both passages make the clear witness that the source of faith is God.*

Matthew 16:3-20. *"Flesh and blood has not revealed this to you, but my Father who is in heaven."*

Hebrews 11. *"Now faith is the assurance of things hoped for, the conviction of things not seen."*

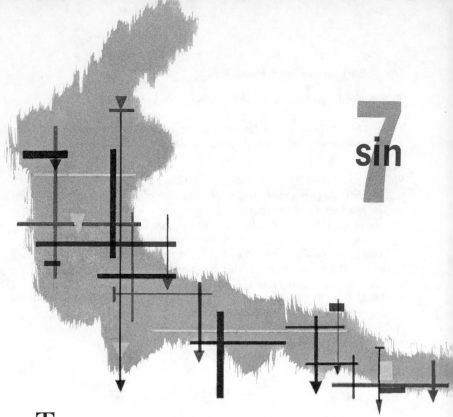

7 sin

T.S. Eliot in his verse drama, *Murder in the Cathedral,* has provided us with helpful insights into the nature of sin. Thomas à Becket, servant of the king, becomes Archbishop of Canterbury and seeks to take his new office with utmost seriousness. Knowing that his actions will lead inevitably to his death, Thomas is tormented by the sin of pride in his own approaching martyrdom. (He is murdered in the Cathedral by four of the king's henchmen.)

> Now is my way clear, now is the meaning plain:
> Temptation shall not come in this kind again.
> The last temptation is the greatest treason:
> To do the right deed for the wrong reason.
> The natural vigour in the venial sin
> Is the way in which our lives begin.

....

Ambition comes when early force is spent
And when we find no longer all things possible.
Ambition comes behind and unobservable.
Sin grows with doing good.*

At the end of the play, the chorus of townspeople make their confession:

Forgive us, O Lord, we acknowledge ourselves as type of the
common man,
Of the men and women who shut the door and sit by the fire;
Who fear the injustice of men less than the justice of God;
Who fear the blessing of God, the loneliness of the night of
God, the surrender required, the deprivation inflicted;
Who fear the hand at the window, the fire in the thatch, the
fist in the tavern, the push into the canal,
Less than we fear the love of God.
We acknowledge our trespass, our weakness, our fault: we
acknowledge
That the sin of the world is upon our heads; that the blood of
the martyrs and the agony of the saints
Is upon our heads.
Lord, have mercy upon us....†

These passages point to the root of the Christian conception of sin. Thomas is tempted to do the right thing for the wrong reason; to satisfy his own ambitions by becoming a martyr.

The sin of the townspeople found expression in a different way. Without the courage to attempt great things, they saved themselves the sin of pride, but suffered the inglorious sin of failure to reprove injustice or to fight righteous battles.

The Knowledge of Sin

Now we know that whatever the law says it speaks to those
who are under the law, so that every mouth may be stopped,
and the whole world may be held accountable to God. For

*T.S. Eliot, *Murder in the Cathedral* (New York: Harcourt, Brace, 1935), p. 196. By permission.

†*Ibid.*, p. 221.

51

no human being will be justified in his sight by works of the law since through the law comes knowledge of sin (Romans 3:19-20).

This relationship of sin, the law, and the knowledge of sin is often given expression in Paul's epistles. The point is an obvious one. A child does not experience the wrongness of an act until the counter-command of the parent calls this knowledge into being. The term conscience does not mean an inherited and unchanging concept of right and wrong. Rather, conscience describes the learned values held by an individual. The law instructs the conscience and also calls forth the knowledge of the rightness or wrongness of an act.

In Christian teaching this becomes a major function of the law of creation and of the revealed law of the Old Testament. The law is given as our custodian, as Paul puts it. We can rejoice in the law, because it holds man in check and provides a measure of order in the midst of an otherwise chaotic society.

But if the law of God brings knowledge of sin, what of the love of God? His love is a two-edged sword. With one edge it destroys us and with the other edge it sets us free. There are few things worse than to realize that we have violated the love of another for us. The man who is unfaithful to a shrew may suffer the conviction that he has broken God's law, or the laws of society. But the man who is unfaithful to a loving wife finds it almost impossible to face that love. The prospect of being forgiven can be worse than the prospect of a barrage of condemnation. The very love which absolves him will first work in him a terrible repentance.

Our knowledge of sin is not simply a matter of hearing the law of the Old Testament. It is, for Christians, the disclosure of the suffering love of God. It is in the cross that we are awakened to the fullest meaning of both sin and grace.

Sin as Condition

And [Isaiah] said: "Woe is me! For I am lost; for I am a man of unclean lips, and I dwell in the midst of a people of

52

unclean lips; for my eyes have seen the King, the LORD of hosts!" (Isaiah 6:5).

But when Simon Peter saw it, he fell down at Jesus' knees, saying, "Depart from me, for I am a sinful man, O Lord" (Luke 5:8).

In Christian teaching, sin is primarily a state of alienation from God. It is a condition in which man finds himself and out of which come specific acts by which that condition is expressed. Man does not live in Eden, but east of Eden (Genesis 3:24). Isaiah, encountered by God, confesses the condition of lostness. Peter, overwhelmed by Christ, confesses his sinful condition.

This is stated clearly in Article II of the *Augsburg Confession*.

> It is also taught among us that since the fall of Adam all men who are born according to the course of nature are conceived and born in sin. That is, all men are full of evil lust and inclinations from their mother's wombs and are unable by nature to have true fear of God and true faith in God....

In the Order for the Baptism of Infants (*SBH,* p. 242), the following is said:

> Dearly Beloved: Forasmuch as all men are born in sin, and our Saviour Jesus Christ hath said, Except a man be born of Water and of the Spirit, he cannot enter into the kingdom of God...

In the *Small Catechism,* Luther wrote:

> *What does such baptizing with water signify?*
> It signifies that the old Adam in us, together with all sins and evil lusts, should be drowned by daily sorrow and repentance and be put to death....

It should be noted that none of these passages attempts to explain the origin of man's sinfulness other than to indicate indirectly that although man was not created to be sinful, no man ever lived who was sinless. References in the *Augsburg Confession* to conception and birth are not meant to imply that

53

sin comes through an act or process which is sinful. Rather, as the text indicates, from the fact of our humanity we are "unable by nature to have true fear of God and true faith in God."

This is what is meant by original sin. It is our very nature to seek to do our own will and to refuse to yield our lives to our Creator. We do good things as goodness is measured in society. But as T. S. Eliot has confessed, this very goodness is a prime source of pride with which we oppose the claims of God. Sin is a condition, a state of being in rebellion against God.

Sin as Act

> Now the works of the flesh are plain: immorality, impurity, licentiousness, idolatry, sorcery, enmity, strife, jealousy, anger, selfishness, dissension, party spirit, envy, drunkenness, carousing, and the like. I warn you, as I warned you before, that those who do such things shall not inherit the kingdom of God (Galatians 5:19-21).

It is important to remember when reading this text that "flesh" for Paul means man apart from God, man as he is identified with the created order.

All sins are the natural outgrowth of man's sinfulness, his state of being separated from the source of his life, which is God. They are the manifestations of his living death.

In the most basic sense, there is no weighting of our sins. They are all of equal seriousness. All have a common root and all are paid the same wage, which is death (Romans 6:23).

At the same time, in terms of our life in society, it is essential that some crimes carry heavier civil penalties. The measure is always the degree of injustice which the act has accomplished. Even in the church we tend to grade sins, largely because the church is also a social structure which needs to be preserved. In contrast with society, which must measure in terms of justice and civil disruption, the church can also weigh in terms of the disruption of the mission of the church. The state, for example, cannot (or should not) punish blasphemy. But such a

54

sin denies the very basis of the life and mission of the church and cannot be ignored by it.

Sin and Satan

The New Testament has much to say about Satan, or the Devil (Matthew 4:1-11, for instance). There is a lively discussion in the church as to whether the Devil is to be understood as an identifiable center of responsibility (a person) or as a personification of what Paul calls "the hosts of darkness." In either case, it is clear that the Devil is never conceived as an evil god. Neither do those who refuse to personify evil necessarily deny in any way the power of evil.

References and Resources

Aulén, Gustaf. *The Faith of the Christian Church,* pp. 259 ff.
Heinecken, Martin J. *Basic Christian Teachings,* Chapter 4.

See also:
Isaiah 59; Ephesians 2:12; Romans 7; Psalm 51.
Small Catechism: Section Four of The Sacrament of Holy Baptism and the First Commandment.

the gospel and salvation

8

Joseph Wood Krutch, former drama critic and English professor at Columbia, wrote a book in 1929 called *The Modern Temper*. At a time when most men were ecstatically optimistic about the future of man, Krutch prophesied that Western civilization was doomed to a loss of meaning which would take all joy from our technical and scientific progress. Already, he said, modern man had lost all capacity to believe in God. He is also in the process of losing his capacity to believe in love.

Such, in outline, is the process by which is accomplished what has here been called the death of a value. Many of us, not yet old, were born at a time when the religion of love was all but unquestioned, when it seemed to stand more firmly than even the religion of the church, whose foundations science was already known slowly to have undermined. But

56

if we have followed the course of modern thought we have seen it rapidly disintegrate. We have seen how works of which Havelock Ellis's *magnum opus* is a type, claimed love as a legitimate subject for rationalistic consideration, and how, though Ellis himself believed that the superstructure of poetry would remain after its foundations had been subject to rational examination, just as Thomas Huxley believed that the superstructure of Christian morality would stand after the supernatural props had been removed from under it, the mystical values lingered as ghosts for only one generation after rationalism had attacked the mythology upon which they rested.

. . . We have grown used — more than [the Victorians] — to a Godless universe, but we are not yet accustomed to one which is loveless as well, and only when we have so become shall we realize what atheism really means.*

This is the situation to which the gospel is now addressed, and the context within which salvation takes its meaning. We are strange beings. If only we could take our meaning from the elemental struggle to live, if hunting and the struggle with the soil could be a reason for living. Or, if only we could be warriors and rejoice in a strong arm against the foe. But for most of us, this is no longer possible. Let's make no value judgments here. Let us simply admit that only a few of us struggle with the soil. This struggle was once transferred to the business world, but the wide-swinging battle to build financial empires great or small is now carefully controlled so that much is rigged and few are hurt. War is now a dirty business. Modern war is to ancient war what the modern slaughter house is to the huntsman stalking meat for his table. And love, the courtly love of the Victorians, became the substitute for struggle against the soil and the conflict of arms. It was better by far, ennobling man, a game with great reward played according to well-defined and enlightened rules. And now this is largely gone. The mystery of love and marriage has become a book of facts.

*Joseph Wood Krutch, "Love — or the Life and Death of a Value," in *The Modern Temper* (New York: Harcourt, Brace, 1929), pp. 73, 78.

Where is the good news for the well-fed, well-protected, efficient killer and mechanical lover? Where is the golden chalice from which he may drink meaning?

Concerning Man

The predicament of modern man is well known in Christian teaching. It is never assumed that man would be able to live like an animal, unconsciously taking existence from the very struggle to live. Man is never defined apart from his relationship with God. He was made by God and in the image of God, which is to say that man has been given the capacity for self-awareness. This allows him an apparently unique relationship with the rest of creation and the Creator. It also means that he is dependent for his continuance upon his maker. And at the heart of man is the capacity to wonder who he is, what his life is about, and where he is going, as well as the capacity to face the fact of his own death. This is the demand for meaning. The demand is not satisfied by fulfillment of the need for food and shelter, for when those needs are met, the question still remains. The demand for meaning is not satisfied by clash of arms, for war no longer has any capacity to give meaning to life, even if it once temporarily served. The demand for meaning is not satisfied by love when love has lost its mystery.

The Christian witness is that the modern predicament is the inevitable result of man's denial of the true source of meaning. Who am I? I am the creature of him whose voice shatters the cedars of Lebanon as he calls me to obedience. He is my God and I am his servant. So long as he is, I am. If I do not know this elemental fact about myself, I have no lasting source of meaning for my living, and my dying is only anxiety and dread, for it too is without meaning.

Hopeless

In some respects, it makes no sense to say that the meaning of our life is found in God. He demands total surrender to himself, and this we cannot do. Our life may be filled with anxiety and dullness, but we cling tenaciously to whatever allows us to say, "I am this or that." We hold this small log in the midst of a great ocean, and we are not about to surrender it for a voice which calls a promise of life.

The Rebirth of Hope

Therefore, since we are justified by faith, we have peace with God through our Lord Jesus Christ. Through him we have obtained access to this grace in which we stand and we rejoice in our hope of sharing the glory of God.... And hope does not disappoint us, because God's love has been poured into our hearts through the Holy Spirit which has been given to us.

While we were yet helpless, at the right time Christ died for the ungodly.... God shows his love for us in that while we were yet sinners Christ died for us (Romans 5:1-8).

The gospel, the good news, is that God himself has restored man to himself in Jesus Christ. The gospel is that God has saved man from the hopelessness of his own incapacity to save himself. The Christian witness is that God came among men in Jesus Christ and while men were still alienated and helpless to let go of other securities, he announced a love which would not give them up. For Christians, who have themselves been in desperate search for meaning, God is no longer one about whom others have spoken. God is the one who continues to make the absolute demand for surrender, and then comes into the world to save us. The Christ in whom God did and suffered these things was raised from the dead. Christians are the people who find in this resurrection the new beginning for mankind, the rescue from hopelessness, the knowledge that God has done what they could not do.

In the formal language of the *Augsburg Confession* (Articles IV and V), it is said in this way:

It is also taught among us that we cannot obtain forgiveness of sin and righteousness before God by our own merits, works, or satisfactions, but that we receive forgiveness of sin and become righteous before God by grace, for Christ's sake, through faith, when we believe that Christ suffered for us and that for his sake our sin is forgiven and righteousness and eternal life are given to us. . . .

To obtain such faith God instituted the office of the ministry, that is, provided the Gospel and the sacraments. Through these, as through means, he gives the Holy Spirit, who works faith, when and where he pleases, in those who hear the Gospel.

References and Resources

Aulén, Gustaf. *The Faith of the Christian Church*, Part III, Section 26.
Heinecken, Martin J. *Basic Christian Teachings*, Chapter 7.
Krutch, Joseph Wood. *The Modern Temper.* New York: Harcourt, Brace, 1929.
   This book is easily read and is written by one of the more literate, and reluctant, atheists of our time.
Wolf, William J. *No Cross, No Crown*, Chapter 3.

See also:
John 3; John 5; Luke 15; Ephesians 2–3; Matthew 28.
Small Catechism: Article Two of the Creed.
Augsburg Confession: Article XVIII.
Service Book and Hymnal: Gloria in Excelsis, p. 3.

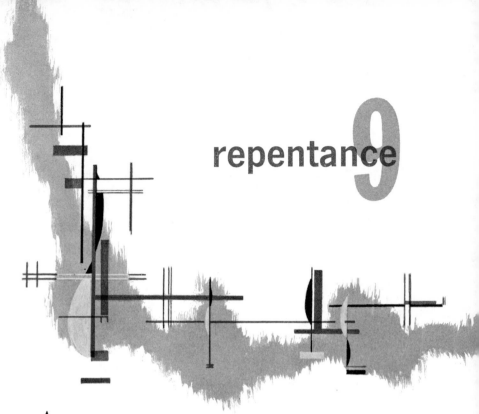

repentance 9

Albert Camus, the French existentialist, was entirely consistent in his atheism. In his novel *The Stranger*, the main character Meursault commits what might be called murder without premeditation, but is nevertheless condemned to death. When the priest comes to see him in his cell, Meursault informs him that he does not believe in God, and that he finds no reason to confess his sins.

> Then, I don't know how it was, but something seemed to break inside me, and I started yelling at the top of my voice. I hurled insults at [the priest], I told him not to waste his rotten prayers on me; it was better to burn than to disappear. I'd taken him by the neckband of his cassock, and, in a sort of ecstasy of joy and rage, I poured out on him all the thoughts that had been simmering in my brain. He seemed so cocksure, you see. And yet none of his certainties was worth one

strand of a woman's hair.... It might look as if my hands were empty. Actually, I was sure of myself, sure about everything, far surer than he; sure of my present life and of the death that was coming.... From the dark horizon of my future a sort of slow, persistent breeze had been blowing toward me, all my life long, from the years that were to come. And on its way that breeze had leveled out all the ideas that people tried to foist on me.... What difference could they make to me, the deaths of others, or a mother's love, or his God?... And what difference could it make if, after being charged with murder, he were executed because he didn't weep at his mother's funeral, since it all came to the same thing in the end? The same thing for Salamano's wife and for Salamano's dog....°

Meursault is not a noble figure, boldly dying for wrongs he did not commit. He is not a tragic figure, suffering the just deserts of his wrongs. He is a modern man portrayed by an existentialist—a man who cannot repent, because he is conscious of no great wrongs. And he knows no great wrongs because he has no knowledge of God and does not accept the values of those who say that they do. For him, repentance has, in fact, no meaning.

Repentance Apart from Christ

It was a far different situation to which John the Baptist spoke:

[John] said therefore to the multitudes that came out to be baptized by him, "You brood of vipers. Who warned you to flee from the wrath to come? Bear fruits that befit repentance, and do not begin to say to yourselves, 'We have Abraham as our father'; for I tell you, God is able from these stones to raise up children to Abraham. Even now the ax is laid to the root of the trees; every tree therefore that does not bear good fruit is cut down and thrown into the fire" (Luke 3:7-9).

°Albert Camus, *The Stranger* (New York: Knopf, 1940), pp. 151-152. By permission.

Instead of saying, "Sorry John, but we don't believe in God," the people said, "What then shall we do?" These were believing Jews to whom John spoke. They were the people of the God who had brought them up out of Egypt, the people who owed allegiance to him and obedience to his law. When John said, "Repent and show the fruits of repentance," their question was "Where do we begin?" not "What's it all about?"

It is wrong to say that the Jews had no concept of the love of God and could not understand sin as offense against this love. But it is true to say that this was a theme subordinate to the relationship defined by the law. It was the breaking of the law which marked their offense; repentance meant to acknowledge this and return to obedience. "Tax collectors also came to be baptized, and said to him, 'Teacher, what shall we do?' And he said to them, 'Collect no more than is appointed you'" (Luke 3:12-13).

John's message was a challenge to do what they knew was rightly expected. Repentance meant contrition and turning again to right actions, the righteousness which God required. But this depends upon an acknowledgment that God does indeed exist and lays against man the claims of the law.

The message of repentance which John preached makes sense to most of us because we also acknowledge God's claim upon us. But we must wonder whether such a message has meaning to the increasing number in the contemporary world for whom God simply does not exist, just as it had no meaning for Meursault.

There are, however, large numbers of people who live by high ethical standards which they profess to be undergirded only by man's need for such ethical living if society is to be maintained. Repentance, for them, has a purely secular meaning: "You must stop living to the detriment of society. Repent and turn to the ethic which is required of our social existence."

But this is not at all what is meant by John the Baptist. Repentance is a turning again to the obligations of the law of God. The baptism which John performed was a washing which symbolized a recommitment to one's obligations to God.

Repentance can have no meaning at all to Camus' Meursault. To the contemporary humanist, it can mean a return to the necessary social standards. It can mean a return to the law of God to the Jew and to the Christian who is limited to moralism in his Christian understanding. But to the Christian who knows the dynamic character of faith, repentance has still fuller meaning.

Repentance and Faith in Christ

It is unprofitable to be too dogmatic about the relationship of repentance and faith. Does a man first repent and then come to faith? Or is it the knowledge which faith gives which works repentance? There is evidence for the first relationship in passages such as this one from Paul's sermon at Corinth: "The times of ignorance God overlooked, but now he commands all men everywhere to repent, because he has fixed a day on which he will judge the world in righteousness by a man whom he has appointed...." But even here, the gospel appears in the balance of the sentence: "and of this he has given assurance to all men by raising him from the dead" (Acts 17:30-31). This same relationship between the demand for repentance and the good news of the gospel is also expressed in Romans 2:4-5, Luke 24:47, 2 Peter 3:9, and Acts 2:37. This relationship is also expressed in Article XII of the *Augsburg Confession:*

> ... Properly speaking, true repentance is nothing else than to have contrition and sorrow, or terror, on account of sin, and yet at the same time to believe the Gospel and absolution (namely, that sin has been forgiven and grace has been obtained through Christ), and this faith will comfort the heart and again set it at rest....

This is surely the way it must be in Christian witness. We do not know the law primarily as a patterned approach to God which can be followed with perseverance and faithfulness.

64

We know the command to love as God has loved us in Christ.

But we know more than the command of love which comes in Christ. We know also the forgiveness which God grants in him. Could we really face the full implication of the command to love as God loves if we did not also hear the word of forgiveness? "True repentance is to have . . . terror . . . and yet at the same time to believe the Gospel and absolution. . . ."

But in Christian teaching, repentance is a turning which results from the total impact of the love of God in Christ. Part of this is the command that we love as we have been loved, and the forgiveness announced in Christ's death and resurrection. Within this context the Holy Spirit calls forth faith, and repentance is a part of this response.

Daily Repentance

Article XII of the *Augsburg Confession* contains the following assertions and refutations:

> It is taught among us that those who sin after Baptism receive forgiveness of sin whenever they come to repentance, and absolution should not be denied them by the church. . . . Rejected here are those who teach that persons who have once become godly cannot fall again.
>
> Condemned on the other hand are the Novations who denied absolution to such as had sinned after Baptism.

The only justification for saying that repentance is not a daily necessity is to say that the Christian man does not sin. But we know that this is not the case. Our relationship with God is restored, but we daily fall away in faithlessness, turning again to other things and people for the source of our life. So, as Karl Barth says, we are always under the necessity of confessing the day's sins and looking back to our Baptism where God's forgiveness is declared. Notice that this is not a matter of racking up all the sins of our youth. They have been confessed and forgiven. It is a matter of acknowledging that sin, the sin which is at work in our very nature, has brought forth new sins. These we acknowledge with contrition and we joyfully receive the absolution — the announcement that we are forgiven. Repentance, like the faith from which it springs, marks both the beginning and the continuance of our life in Christ.

Postscript

It must not be assumed from what has been said that only the repentance born of faith has meaning. It may be the breaking of what one considers only the civil law which awakens the desire to reorient one's life. In this situation, a man may hear the gospel with new ears and the repentance which is born of faith in Christ then supplants the repentance born of an infraction of the civil law.

It is also true, as has been said before, that Christian teaching does not instruct us to sit down and wait for the Spirit to call forth the response of repentance and faith. The indifference marked by "sitting down" is the least fertile ground for the work of the Spirit. Rise up and shake your fist at the heavens, or rise up and determine to follow the law. Either action leaves one open to the work which God would do in us.

References and Resources

Aulén, Gustaf. *The Faith of the Christian Church,* Part IIIb, Section 34.

Barth, Karl. *Dogmatics in Outline.* New York: Harper Torchbooks, 1959, Chapter 23.

Heinecken, Martin J. *Basic Christian Teachings,* Chapter 8.

See also:
Small Catechism: Section Four of The Sacrament of Holy Baptism.
Hosea 1–3. *A study in repentance worked by God.*

forgiveness 10

One of the most comforting, and yet most disturbing, parables in the New Testament is the one which begins:

> And [Jesus] said, "There was a man who had two sons; and the younger of them said to his father, 'Father, give me the share of property that falls to me.' And he divided his living between them. Not many days later, the younger son gathered all he had and took his journey into a far country, and there he squandered his property in loose living" (Luke 15:11-13).

This parable is comforting to whatever extent we have been younger sons spending our substance in riotous living in a far country. It is disturbing to whatever extent we are also elder brothers, incredulous at such rich gifts to those so much less worthy than we.

No excuse is offered for the younger son. He squanders his wealth in immoral ways and is reduced to utter poverty. There seems to be no great soul-searching as he simply contemplates the fact that his father's servants are eating, and he is not. There just is not much in the parable to his credit.

The crux of the parable is in the action which occurs as the young reprobate approaches his home. "But while he was yet at a distance, his father saw him and had compassion, and ran and embraced him and kissed him" (Luke 15:20). No sackcloth and ashes. Not even a waiting for the speech which any father would know to be forthcoming. This was an amazing example of a love which rushes forward to forgive.

It was an offensive action, too—the action of a sentimental old fool whose love has bounced out of touch with reality and has worked injustice. So at least, it seemed to the eldest, the hardworking, honest, stay-at-home son.

It is a joy to preach this parable of God's forgiveness to men chained by the conviction of their sin. But can it be defended against the caustic comments of more objective critics?

The Radical Character of Forgiveness

The radical character of God's forgiveness in Christian teaching becomes clear in the light of the witness concerning the nature of both sin and grace.

That which is forgiven is sin in its most profound sense. In the parable of the prodigal, it would be possible to make light of the offense. An immature son has his fling at the world and, as his father fully expected, comes back, having learned his lesson. But sin in Christian teaching is a turning of one's back on God the Father, not just a momentary lapse from the rules of the house or the committing of a season of indiscretion. It is the rejection of a person, the spurning of the loving Father himself. It is necessary to imagine something like a wise and devoted father who instructs his son not to drive over a safe speed when he takes his sister to the store. The son laughs in his father's face and calls him an old fool. He speeds to the

68

store, fails to stop at an intersection, and his sister is maimed for life. This is the nature of the sin which is forgiven.

The nature of God's grace is also to be understood in its most radical sense. That is, God forgives without being conditional. When the son comes home with the horrible news of his sister's maiming, the father waits for him with forgiveness in his heart and on his tongue. Perhaps this is where the modern parable fails us. No earthly father could stand there waiting with forgiveness in his heart. But this is the testimony concerning God. He does not wait for us to speak our confession, but comes forward with a forgiving heart and word untouched by sarcasm or cold restraint.

Nothing can be said to temper the incomprehensible character of such an act. Men forgive things done in ignorance. God forgives also when the sin is conscious and deliberate. Men forgive when, in their own need, they forgive to have back the one needed. God, in contrast to man, is not dependent upon the one loved. Men forgive because they know themselves to be sinners and see themselves in the acts of another. God has no such need for tolerance. Men forgive when they lose a standard for measuring things good and bad, and forgiveness can have no meaning. God has not lost this capacity to judge.

There is no tempering of the radical character of forgiveness. God is both unflinchingly set against man's self-love and disobedience, and at the same time forgiving, reconciling man unto himself without demanding any sort of payment.

It is clear, then, that God's forgiveness is not an act of justice. Justice requires that each man receive what is rightfully his. According to justice, each man would be required to pay the rightful penalty for his offense. In Christian teaching, the sinner receives the gift of forgiveness without paying a penalty.

Charges Against the Teaching

One of the objections to this doctrine is that the sinner gets off too easily. Consider, however, the earlier example of the son who has maimed his sister. If he were confronted by his father's forgiveness, would he in fact consider this an easy experience? More likely, it would be the source of a repentance more thoroughgoing than any beating or disownment. Most of us would rather be dealt with according to some kind of justice which allows us eventually to feel that we have paid off the debt.

We have missed the meaning of being loved in this way if we assume that being forgiven is easy. It works in us a total reorientation from self-acceptance and brings us to a total dependence upon God's acceptance of us. Such a wrenching of one's life is a shaking experience. Such repentance, or turning about, is not a precondition to God's forgiveness, but the result of such forgiveness. If we speak casually about being forgiven, we are surely innocent of its full meaning.

The second charge against this teaching is that it denies the tragic character of sin. In the parable, this is in part the charge of the eldest son. In the case of the son who maims his sister, the charge would be that the father's forgiveness makes light of the enormity of what has happened.

But this charge can hardly be made against God. The cost of such forgiveness is demonstrated in the cross of Jesus Christ. Perhaps we have some idea of what a father suffers when a son leaves home and destroys himself. Or perhaps we have some idea of what it costs a father to have his son reject him and harm his daughter. Such understanding should allow us to see the cross as a measure of the cost of God's love for men. The forgiveness which God offers is not without its price, and it is God who pays it. God allows man's sin and death to impinge upon God's own life, for he allowed his Son to suffer and die.

Justification and Forgiveness

The average twentieth-century Christian has some difficulties with the word justification. In everyday language it means "I was right all the time and this has now been proven." Obviously, this is not what St. Paul meant when he wrote "Then what becomes of our boasting? It is excluded. On what principle? On the principle of works? No, but on the principle of faith. For we hold that a man is justified by faith apart from the works of the law" (Romans 3:27-28).

The meaning of justification in the biblical sense is that a man is restored to his proper place in the household of God. In other words, man is forgiven. We who were alienated and separated from God by our sin and sinning have been restored by God's act of forgiveness. And this forgiveness is solely a gift of God's love, received through faith. Even the faith with which we receive the gift is worked in us by God through his Holy Spirit. This is what is meant by the confession that we are justified by grace through faith alone.

Forgiven and Forgiving

> Put on then, as God's chosen ones, holy and beloved, compassion, kindness, lowliness, meekness, and patience, forbearing one another and, if one has a complaint against another, forgiving each other; as the Lord has forgiven you, so you also must forgive (Colossians 3:12-13).

Forgiveness is not only the way by which God restores us unto himself, but also the means by which men are to share in the redemptive work of Christ. As we have been forgiven, we also are to forgive those who offend against us. Dietrich Bonhoeffer defined the church as forgiven people learning how to forgive. Our life is God's gift. We are, therefore, free to forgive, for our lives are not threatened by transgressions against us.

References and Resources

Aulén, Gustaf. *The Faith of the Christian Church*, pp. 288-314.
Heinecken, Martin J. *Basic Christian Teachings*, pp. 83-84.

See also:
Matthew 18:21-22. *The unlimited character of forgiveness.*
Matthew 9:1-8. *The relationship of forgiveness and healing.*
Small Catechism: Fifth Petition of the Lord's Prayer.
Augsburg Confession, Article IV. *We receive forgiveness by grace.*

the communion of saints

11

Jean-Paul Sartre in his play, *No Exit*, tells us that when an individual is dependent upon other people he is in hell. The Christian teaching is that men are indeed dependent upon other men. Sartre concludes that no man should be dependent upon other men.

No Exit is set in a room without windows. Three people inhabit the room: Garcin, who is a coward; Inez, who is homosexual; and Estelle, who killed her child. Estelle is vain and needs a looking glass. Inez offers to be her mirror and Estelle replies, "But how can I rely upon your taste? Is it the same as *my* taste? . . . You scare me rather. My reflection in the glass never did that; of course, I knew it so well. Like something I had tamed. . . . I'm going to smile, and my smile will sink down into your pupils, and heaven knows what it will become."

Estelle needs Inez, but Inez will destroy her. Garcin needs Estelle, but Estelle is repulsed by his cowardice. Inez needs Estelle, but Garcin thwarts her. Garcin concludes, "So this is hell. I'd never have believed it. You remember all we were told about the torture-chambers, the fire and brimstone, the 'burning marl.' Old wives tales! There's no need for red-hot pokers. Hell is — other people!"*

We really know this, and we take it seriously, but we still talk bravely about our individual freedom. There is no individualism apart from our life in community. Our ability to say "I" grows out of our relationship with others who are already saying "I." A child reared completely apart from other human beings gives no indication of the kind of self-transcendence which we describe as being the mark of man. We are not individuals who happen to enjoy living together. We are self-conscious individuals *because* we are established in community.

Sartre understands the terrible possibility of such dependence upon one another. If we are dependent upon what others think of us for our self-image, how crucial it becomes that others give us a true reflection of ourselves. Or, if not a true image, at least one with which we can live. The most horrible line in the play is spoken by Inez to Estelle: "I'll be nice to you, ever so nice. Only you must be nice to me, too."† This is the game in which we are all involved. We depend upon others for love and status and a self-image with which we can live. They are dependent, to a greater or lesser degree, upon us. We will please them, but they must please us. And together we live in relationships which are indeed hell — destructive, dishonest, false, and tragic.

Christian teaching denies none of this, but it has much to add. Man is created to live in community, but also in fellowship with the God who created us to live in community. I and

*Jean-Paul Sartre, *No Exit and The Flies* (New York: Knopf, 1954), pp. 26-27.

†*Ibid.*, p. 28.

my neighbor, apart from God, destroy one another. Only as both my neighbor and I take our lives from our relationship with the God who does not need us will we be free in our relationship with one another. This is the distinctive characteristic of the church, the communion of saints.

The Nature of the Church

It is also taught among us that one holy Christian church will be and remain forever. This is the assembly of all believers among whom the Gospel is preached in its purity and the holy sacraments are administered according to the Gospel ... (*Augsburg Confession,* Article VII).

So then you are no longer strangers and sojourners, but you are fellow citizens with the saints and members of the household of God, built upon the foundation of the apostles and prophets, Christ Jesus himself being the chief cornerstone, in whom the whole structure is joined together and grows into a holy temple in the Lord; in whom you also are built into it for a dwelling place of God in the Spirit (Ephesians 2:19-21).

Sociologists rightly study the church as one of the many institutions within society. In most cases it appears to be a free association, something which one may join, or from which he may separate himself. Whether or not an individual does either depends upon his needs.

The Christian understands the sociologist's description, but must go on to say that there are things which the sociologist, as sociologist, is unable to comprehend. In Christian understanding, the church is essentially a communion of saints. Men and women who were "strangers and sojourners" in the land of death where men destroy one another in the struggle for selfhood have been restored to the source of life. The restoration is effected through the act of God in Jesus Christ, the witness of those sent (the apostles) to proclaim this act (the gospel), and the work of God the Spirit who calls us to know its truth and rightful claim (faith). When we call ourselves saints, we do not mean that we have become perfect, but only that, in spite of our sins, we have been forgiven and restored to God.

So the Christian does not consider the church something which he joins or leaves at will. It is first of all a relationship into which he is called by the Holy Spirit. But this relationship with God, by which he becomes a saint, is at the same time a relationship with other saints. This is more than a matter of individuals who have had a common experience. All who have traveled in Europe have something in common, and they might join a "European Travelers' Club." This is not the kind of relationship which Christians have to one another, since we are not joined by a tangential concern, but rather have been given a common source for our lives. We are the blocks of a building, all dependent upon the one cornerstone, which is Christ (Ephesians 2:19-21). We are all members of one body, each having a different function, but all having the same head, which is Christ (1 Corinthians 12:12-27). Our individual life is taken from one source of life, which is God the Father (Ephesians 4:1-7).

There is another sense in which we are more than an association of saved individuals. Our individual restoration to God has been effected through the church. We are not saved (rescued from the death of our alienation from God) apart from the witness to God's act in Christ. This witness has come to us from the church, the communion of saints. The church is, therefore, our mother. Every Christian confesses this common mother and consequently that he is brother and sister to every other Christian. This is a theological concept, not just a hope that we can be like brothers. The term fellowship no longer does justice to the Greek word *koinonia,* which implies a common source for the life of the group, not simply the holding of similar interests.

The Life of the Church

The members of the body of Christ have been forgiven (accepted and restored) by God. They do not depend upon other men to provide a true image of themselves. They need not pervert themselves in order to have the favor of other men. This sets the Christian free from the kind of hell described by Sartre. The Christian then freely becomes the servant of his neighbors, and in this act also liberates the neighbor. In fact, this freely given service becomes the soil within which the witness to God's self-giving to men can be planted.

This is what the gospel means for our life together, but it is obvious that it does not find fulfillment in our life as it is. So we encounter once again the basic paradox in Christian teaching. We are both saved and sinners. We are a new community which nevertheless lives too much in the old ways. And the resolution of this dilemma is the continuing forgiveness which allows us to press on with joy, and the promise of the eventual end of the conflict which allows us to press on with hope.

As indicated in the *Augsburg Confession,* the life of the church is nourished by the preaching of the Word, which is the continued witness to Christ, and by the sacraments, which are embodiments of the Word. The worship of the church and her service in the world are the visible response which faith makes to the proclamation of the gospel.

The church lives within institutional forms. The church is not of the world, but it is in the world. It therefore requires the structures by which things in the world are ordered. Someone must set the time when the people shall gather for worship and someone must decide who shall preach the Word, or whether the preaching is indeed the witness given by the apostles. Be it simple or elaborate, structural form is essential to the life of the church. The question is not whether the communion of saints shall have institutional form, but whether or not the existing form serves its proper function.

The Church and Christ

The church is the continuing incarnation of Christ, God's revelation. Its worship is centered in the cycle of remembrance by which his life, death, and resurrection are proclaimed. In the fulfillment of its mission, the church carries on the redemptive work of Christ. The people of the church are *saints* through Christ. The people of the church are a *communion* of saints as they are in Christ and are nourished in him. The lordship of Christ is manifest to the world in the church, and in the church the risen Christ reigns.

Since the church has its life through Christ and lives in Christ, the church is one, just as Christ is one. The oneness of the church is given by Christ. The division of the church is the work of men. The church is catholic (or universal, or ecumenical) because it is one body in Christ and has a mission to all the world. This is true even when the church at any given time is also divided and fails to fulfill its mission. It is agreed that the division of the church is a denial of its Lord—it is sinful. This is again our basic dualism. Saved men are still sinful; saved people are one in Christ and yet divided. The resolution of the dilemma is the same: the divided church rejoices in forgiveness, strives for unity, and expects to be made whole.

References and Resources

Aulén, Gustaf. *The Faith of the Christian Church*, pp. 329-353.
Barth, Karl. *Dogmatics in Outline*, Chapter 22.
Heinecken, Martin J. *Basic Christian Teachings*, Chapter 9.

See also:
Ephesians 1:1; Romans 1:7; 1 Corinthians 1:2; Philippians 4:21 *(Salutations to the saints).*
Colossians 3:12-17; John 15 *(Vine and branches).*
The Epistle to the Hebrews. *A reading of this will provide rich content for the outline given in this chapter.*
Large Catechism, the Third Article of the Creed. *Luther's explanation is a basic witness to the work of the Holy Spirit in the life of the church.*

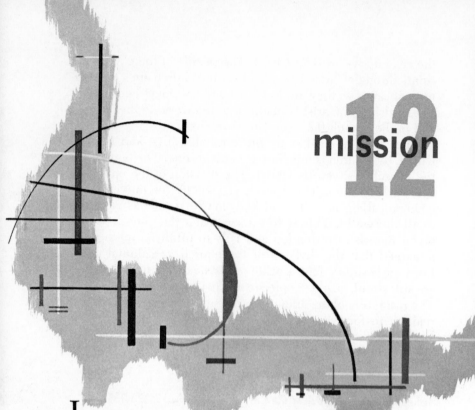

mission 12

In order to speak of what the church is, it is necessary to speak of what the church does. Just as we know God only in his acts, we can know the church only in the things which it is called to do. Our Lord sent his disciples to all the nations to baptize and teach (Matthew 28:19-20). This was to be the work of the church. The full implications of this commission are nowhere given more cogent expression than in these words:

> From now on, therefore, we regard no one from a human point of view; even though we once regarded Christ from a human point of view, we regard him thus no longer. Therefore, if any one is in Christ, he is a new creation; the old has passed away, behold, the new has come. All this is from God, who through Christ reconciled us to himself and gave us the ministry of reconciliation; that is, God was in Christ reconciling the world to himself, not counting their trespasses

against them, and entrusting to us the message of reconciliation. So we are ambassadors for Christ, God making his appeal through us. We beseech you on behalf of Christ, be reconciled to God. For our sake he made him to be sin who knew no sin, so that in him we might become the righteousness of God (2 Corinthians 5:16-21).

In Christ, a new creation has taken place, a new beginning. The church is a new people, reconciled to God through Christ, and called to a ministry of reconciliation. God will continue to make himself known in and through these people as they accomplish this ministry. The church came into being on Pentecost, the day on which the preaching started (Acts 2).

This understanding of mission was strong in the church's earliest years and found manifestation in later centuries in such men as Augustine, Boniface, and Ansgar, who spread the gospel beyond the borders of the Roman world. Even in the time when the church was caught up in its struggle to dominate the temporal powers, orders of preaching monks continued to carry out this mission. The Reformation represented the church's mission to itself and flowered in a rebirth of preaching and missionary activity which reached a peak in the massive missionary efforts of the nineteenth century. By the middle of the twentieth century, the church found itself threatened by the religious character of a new nationalism and the indifference of the new science. Under the impact of these threats, the church has come once again to the recognition that its life is centered in its mission. However, the meaning of mission has grown beyond the image of a missionary sent to a far place, and the word mission now embraces the totality of the church's life. This broadened understanding of mission is the subject of this chapter.

The Church and Celebration

In listing the duties to Christian people, Paul wrote, "Let the word of Christ dwell in you richly, as you teach and admonish one another in all wisdom, and as you sing psalms and hymns and spiritual songs with thankfulness in your hearts to God" (Colossians 3:16). So also the writer to the Hebrews: "Through him then let us continually offer up a sacrifice of praise to God, that is, the fruit of lips that acknowledge his name" (Hebrews 13:15). This is not a rite which we are commanded to perform. It is the response of praise and thanksgiving, the celebration of acts of God already accomplished in Christ. The service which we render unto God is precisely this offering of prayer, praise, and thanksgiving. This is work done by the people of God, a part of the church's mission in the world. The joy expressed for our own reconciliation becomes a witness to him. Worship is the doing of what comes unbidden from our hearts.

When we consider worship as a means of keeping the family together or of providing the children with a code of ethics, we deny the true nature of worship. This has tended to separate worship and mission, and each has suffered from the division. It is impossible to understand worship as a part of the church's mission if we see it as something other than or less than celebration.

The Household of Faith

> And let us not grow weary in well-doing, for in due season we shall reap, if we do not lose heart. So then, as we have opportunity, let us do good to all men, and especially to those who are of the household of faith (Galatians 6:9-10).

Christians are sometimes embarrassed by this reference to the household of faith and the many like it in the New Testament. On the surface, it seems a little exclusive. And while we may practice exclusiveness, it is seldom commended openly. But there is an exclusiveness about the church. It is made up of those who confess that Jesus Christ is Lord, that God alone is the source of life and that he has given us this life through Jesus Christ. The church is made up of all those who confess that the truth of this is known to them through faith. It is reasonable to expect that those whose whole life is thus reoriented should have much in common. They have a common Lord, desire a common obedience, offer a common worship, and live in a common hope. Therefore, the way in which they love one another, resolve difficulties, administer their affairs, rear their children, and serve one another ought to reflect the single ultimate concern to which each is committed. The life which is lived within the household of faith will inevitably make a witness to the world. Attention to this inner life of the church, the edification of the people of God, becomes therefore an essential part of the mission of the church.

The Ministry of Reconciliation

In addition to the witness of its worship and the witness of its common life, the church is called to preach the gospel, to proclaim the forgiveness of God in Christ. Something quite particular is meant by this. In its basic and fullest sense, it means a man or a woman proclaiming in person the things which God has done in Christ. The gospel in print, preaching by radio and television, and the use of visual aids are all secondary and derivative forms of what is meant here. There is no substitute for the encounter of persons in which the Word becomes incarnate in direct speech.

The poor quality of the preaching of some and the attempted manipulation of people exhibited by others have both tended to obscure the fact that preaching or witness is still the instrument of the Holy Spirit for winning the response of faith. It is practiced, to be sure, within our church buildings, but it is shunned as somehow unethical in our personal encounters. The renewed interest in mission which has marked the mid-twentieth century has resulted in a large number of efforts by small groups to learn how to make this kind of witness.

The mission of the church is also accomplished as a work of redemption within the orders of society. In some respects this is the work of picking up the pieces of a fragmented society. Just as Christ ministered to the total needs of the outcasts of his society, the church has sought to fulfill a similar responsibility in the centuries which have followed. The care of the poor, the widow, the orphan, the sick, and the aged have been major concerns. This kind of service is understood by the church to be something more than an act of good will or a way to win men to Christ, though it has been this, too. It has been a necessity imposed upon the church as it sought to conform its life to the life of Christ, to his self-giving in death and his life-giving in resurrection. It is a joyous undertaking, the work to which the church is called.

The church has also sought to call the state to its task of providing justice and order. In periods when the church has been a strong and direct influence upon the state, the approach has been as direct as Luther telling the prince that he was doing too little about education. Now a minority group within most major nations, the church is seeking to reassess its social responsibility.

The church understands, at least in part, the failure of its mission in the world. At the same time, the church has never been more certain that it has a mission, and that this mission includes the witness of its worship, the witness of its common life, the witness of preaching, and the witness of a many-faceted redemptive ministry to the world.

References and Resources

Aulén, Gustaf. *The Faith of the Christian Church*, pp. 408-426.
Bonhoeffer, Dietrich. *Life Together.* New York: Scribner's, 1948.
Heinecken, Martin J. *Basic Christian Teachings*, Chapters 8 and 9.
Kantonen, T. A. *A Theology of Evangelism.* Philadelphia: Muhlenberg Press, 1954.
Letts, Harold (ed.). *Christian Social Responsibility.* Philadelphia: Muhlenberg Press, 1957. Volume III, Chapters 1 and 6.
Williams, Daniel D. *What Present-Day Theologians Are Thinking.* New York: Harper, rev. ed., 1959. Chapter 5.

See also:
Luke 24:46-48; Acts 1:8; Isaiah 41:8-13; Philippians 2:12-13; John 17:20-21.
Augsburg Confession: Articles IX, XIII, XV, XVI, and XXVIII.

the word

13

The difficulties encountered by the modern Christian with the term Word of God are rooted in the church's multiple use of the term in all of its teaching and preaching. In the *Small Catechism*, for example, we find the following questions and answers:

> *What is Baptism?*
> The Sacrament of Baptism is not water only, but it is water used together with God's Word and by his Command.
> *What is this Word?*
> In Matthew 28, our Lord Jesus Christ says: "Go therefore and make disciples of all nations, baptizing them in the name of the Father and of the Son and of the Holy Spirit."

It is clear that Word of God here refers to words of the Bible. It is something else again in the following quotation from

Article III of the *Augsburg Confession* (Latin Text):

> Our churches also teach that the Word—that is, the Son of God—took on man's nature in the womb of the blessed virgin Mary.

There is no mistaking the intention. The Word is Christ. This use has its roots in the language of the fourth Gospel:

> In the beginning was the Word, and the Word was with God, and the Word was God.... And the Word became flesh and dwelt among us, full of grace and truth; we have beheld his glory, glory as of the only Son from the Father (John 1:1, 14).

So we have become accustomed to speaking of the words of the Bible as the Word of God, and of Christ as the Word of God. We also speak of preaching the Word, by which some mean preaching Christ, others mean preaching the words of the Bible, and many mean both.

There is a legitimate way in which each of these terms can be used, but indiscriminate, interchangeable usage has led to considerable confusion. The ways in which the term Word of God can properly be used are the subject of this chapter.

Christ the Word

The Jews considered a man's name to be the most personal symbol of himself. For this reason, they would not use God's name. Even today, to know a man's name or to be able to call him by name marks a degree of relationship to him. We have a similar concept of the relationship between the words which a man speaks and himself. "His word is as good as his bond" is something which all of us would like to have said of us.

This role of speech as a disclosure of the self was one of the things which prompted the church to call Christ the Word of God. It is not only what Christ said about God, but the totality of his life, death, and resurrection which makes him God's Word to us. He is the Revelation, the self-disclosure of God. He is God's Word.

It is crucial that we understand the dynamic character of this usage. If you look at any word on this page, you have an "it." It is dead in itself. Cut up the page, separate the letters, analyze the origins of the word, do anything you like to it. The word is yours to do with as you will. Of course, it holds a potential as a symbol which can evoke remembrances of living relationships with other people. But a printed word is in itself a derivative thing. It has come out of living relationships.

Christ, the Word of God, is quite different. He is not an "it" and cannot be divided or analyzed. God's self-disclosure allows us to be encountered by a "Thou," a person, and the encounter will always, therefore, be dynamic rather than static. This is the basic meaning of the term Word of God, and all meanings derive from it. God's Word to men is the living Christ.

The Bible and the Word

The Bible has been the only holy book in the life of the church. All of the teaching and worship of Protestant Christianity is rooted in the Bible, and its creeds and confessions claim to be correct expositions of the Bible. But the Bible came out of the life of the church, not the church out of the Bible.

The Christian church was called into being through an act of God by which he disclosed himself in his Word, Jesus Christ. Through this act the Holy Spirit called forth faith in men and gathered them as the church. The remembrance of that which was done and said by Christ was set down in a number of ways, some of which have come to us as the four Gospels. Leaders of the church wrote letters of counsel and admonition to the young congregations. Some of the Gospels and some of the letters were recognized in the church as testimony true to their remembrance of Christ and in accord with the knowledge (faith) called forth in them by the Holy Spirit.

So we begin by defining the Word of God as a message from God to men. The Old Testament is also the Word of God, in that it is God's message to Israel as it has been written down.

But the Word of God became flesh in Jesus Christ and he is God's message to men fulfilling all that was spoken by God to Israel. The New Testament is the writing down of God's self-disclosure in Christ. Therefore, the Old and New Testaments can also be called the Word of God, but they derive from the message spoken by the prophets and from the message which is Christ. The New Testament has become the anchor for all Christian teaching and the guide for all Christian preaching. But we do not confuse the Word which is the living Christ and the words of the Bible which derive from God's act in Christ. Luke's introduction to his Gospel indicates this clearly:

> Inasmuch as many have undertaken to compile a narrative of the things which have been accomplished among us, just as they were delivered to us by those who from the beginning were eyewitnesses and ministers of the word, it seemed good to me also, having followed all things closely for some time past, to write an orderly account for you, most excellent Theophilus, that you may know the truth concerning the things of which you have been informed (Luke 1:1-4).

Luke here indicates that this Gospel will be his own work. But it is not a story which he has invented. It is a recording of the witness of those who had been with Christ from the beginning and of those who in Luke's own time were preaching through the enlightenment and power of the Holy Spirit. In what he wrote, the church found a document which was alive with the same Spirit who had called forth faith in them. The Gospel of Luke grew out of the witness of the church and was found by the church to be in accord with its faith and witness. In turn, Luke's Gospel has nurtured the life and faith of the church in the centuries which have followed.

This, then, is the relationship between the Word which is Christ and the Word which is the Bible. The Bible bears witness to Christ, and Christ is God's own self-disclosure. The truth of Christ and the truth of the witness of the Bible are revealed to us by the Holy Spirit. The truth is known through the eyes of faith. As God was both hidden and revealed in the man Jesus of Nazareth, so the biblical witness to Christ is both

86

hidden and revealed in the language and thought forms of a particular time and place, as men of that time and place put their witness in writing.

The Word, Preaching, and Sacraments

Christ, the Word of God, becomes incarnate (takes flesh) in today's church as witness to him is made in preaching and through the action of Baptism and the Lord's Supper. However, it should be clear that the preaching of the Word finds its roots in the words of the New Testament and that the command and promise for the sacraments are also found in the words of the New Testament. At the same time, it is the Holy Spirit which shows us that the Word which is proclaimed in preaching and in the actions of the sacraments is indeed God revealing himself through his redemptive acts in Christ.

The dynamic interrelationship of Christ, the words of Scripture, preaching, and sacraments is indicated in the following passage from Luther:

> If you are asked: how do you know it? [speaking of Christ's redemptive activity] you should answer: I know it because I hear it in the Word and sacrament and absolution, and because the Holy Spirit says the very same thing in my heart: that is, that Christ became man for me, died, rose again . . . that is, it agrees with the Holy Scriptures, just as the Holy Spirit writes it in your heart.*

So man's total dependence upon God is not relieved in the church's teaching concerning the Word. Christ is God's Word to man, not man's highest expression of himself. The knowledge that this Christ is indeed God's Word to us is a knowledge granted by God the Holy Spirit. When the witness is recorded in the words of the New Testament, it is also a witness to Christ, but knowing of this truth also depends upon the testimony of the Holy Spirit. Christ, the Word, is proclaimed in preaching and in the action of the sacraments. This

*Quoted in Emil Brunner, *The Philosophy of Religion* (New York: Scribner's, 1937), p. 27.

87

proclamation is rooted in the Scriptures, but it is productive of faith in men not because the Scriptures are believed to be infallible, but because the Holy Spirit bears testimony in our hearts that this Scripture—rooted in preaching and sacramental action—is indeed God's disclosure of himself.

References and Resources

Aulén, Gustaf. *The Faith of the Christian Church,* Sections 40-42, pp. 353-378.
> See Aulén's concept of sacraments as action, to which this book is indebted. See also his discussion of "conversation" as a means of grace.

Barth, Karl. *Dogmatics in Outline,* Chapter 10.
> See especially page 67.

Heinecken, Martin J. *Basic Christian Teachings,* pp. 118-122.
Sittler, Joseph A. *The Doctrine of the Word.* Philadelphia: United Lutheran Publishing House, 1948.
> This is a brief but excellent book. It is out of print, but may be found in the pastor's library.

Williams, Daniel D. *What Present-Day Theologians Are Thinking,* Chapter 2.

See also:
2 Peter 1:20; James 1:22; 2 Timothy 4:2; Colossians 3:16.
Small Catechism: Third Article of the Creed and the Third Commandment.

the kingdom of god

14

In the following brief passage from his explanation of the Second Petition of the Lord's Prayer in the *Large Catechism*, Luther gives expression to the threefold character of the kingdom of God:

> What is the kingdom of God? Answer: Simply what we have learned in the Creed, namely, that God sent his Son, Christ our Lord, into the world to redeem and deliver us from the power of the devil and to bring us to himself and rule us as a king of righteousness, life, and salvation against sin, death, and an evil conscience. To this end he also gave his Holy Spirit to teach us this through his holy Word and to enlighten and strengthen us in faith by his power.
>
> We pray here at the outset that all this may be realized in us and that God's name may be praised through his holy Word and our Christian lives. This we ask, both in order that we

who have accepted it may remain faithful and grow daily in it and in order that it may gain recognition and followers among other people and advance with power throughout the world. So we pray that, led by the Holy Spirit, many may come into the kingdom of grace and become partakers of salvation, so that we may all remain together eternally in this kingdom which has now made its appearance among us.

The kingdom of God is a kingdom in which the Christian already lives and grows, it is one which is to be extended, and it is one which will come. The kingdom exists where God now rules and gathers, it will be extended as we fulfill our mission, and it will come to us when time ends. It is difficult to say all of this together because it seems to show a measure of contradiction, but all three are elements in the Christian teaching concerning the kingdom. The purpose of this chapter is not to show how this can be, but to be as clear as possible concerning its meaning.

The Kingdom in the Teaching of Christ

The teaching of Christ concerning the kingdom is indicated in the passages which follow.

> Now after John was arrested, Jesus came into Galilee, preaching the gospel of God, and saying, "The time is fulfilled, and the kingdom of God is at hand; repent, and believe in the gospel" (Mark 1:14-15).

> These twelve Jesus sent out, charging them, "Go nowhere among the Gentiles, and enter no town of the Samaritans, but go rather to the lost sheep of the house of Israel, And preach as you go, saying, 'The kingdom of heaven is at hand'" (Matthew 10:5-7).

The old age was coming to a close, and the new age of God's reign was at hand. It will come as miraculously as the mustard seed becomes a tree. It will come in the same miraculous manner that leaven raises a loaf of bread (Matthew 13:31-33). The coming of the kingdom demands decision. There is no time to bury the dead (Matthew 8:22). "No one who puts his hand to the plow and looks back is fit for the kingdom of God" (Luke 9:62). In parable after parable Jesus indicated the immediacy of this event, the decision demanded, and the readiness required.

There are numerous indications in the Synoptic Gospels that Jesus understood his own ministry as a sign of the coming of the kingdom. When John the Baptist sent his disciples to inquire whether or not Jesus was the Messiah, Jesus simply replied that the signs of the coming reign of God were taking place through him:

> "Go and tell John what you hear and see: the blind receive their sight and the lame walk, lepers are cleansed and the deaf hear, and the dead are raised up, and the poor have good news preached to them. And blessed is he who takes no offense at me" (Matthew 11:4-6).

All of this was said against the background of a struggle between God and the hosts of darkness which were the undoing of the previous age. These were now to be defeated. The crucial battle was fought in Christ himself and through the resurrection he was the firstborn of a new creation, the second Adam (1 Corinthians 15:45-47).

The Kingdom Now

God's reign does not extend to us on the basis that we, like Christ, have been perfectly responsive to the will of God. This has been the teaching of some groups of Christians who have insisted that Jesus was the best of men and that it is our responsibility to rise to his pattern. Paul speaks decisively against this view:

> But now the righteousness of God has been manifested apart from the law, although the law and the prophets bear witness to it, the righteousness of God through faith in Jesus Christ for all who believe. For there is no distinction; since all have sinned and fall short of the glory of God, they are justified by his grace as a gift, through the redemption which is in Christ

91

Jesus, whom God put forward as an expiation by his blood, to be received by faith (Romans 3:21-25).

So we do not walk into the kingdom of God or knock on God's gate and ask for admission to his kingdom. Rather, God comes to us with the gift of Christ's righteousness. To receive this gift is what Paul means by being "in Christ" and to be in Christ, the one in whom God reigns, is to be received also into God's kingdom, to come under God's reign.

This means that we become sons of God by adoption (Galatians 4:1-7), or as alien branches which have been grafted onto the true vine (John 15:1-11). The question is whether or not this is the end of it. Is this what it means to be in the kingdom of God now? Not at all! Now that we are adopted sons, we are to live like sons. Once grafted onto the vine, we are to bear good fruit. Luther writes, "To this end he also gave his Holy Spirit to teach us this through his holy Word and to enlighten and strengthen us in faith by his power."

The Kingdom's Spread

The spread of the reign of God is always a matter of personal growth in grace, the struggle to allow our lives to be conformed to the loving will of God. But it is much more than personal. In Luther's words, it is also to extend the reign of God that it "may gain recognition and followers among other people and advance with power throughout the world."

We should have no illusions about this. There are numerous concepts backed by strong groups, which seek recognition and followers. Both nudism and vegetarianism, for example, are worldwide movements making claims for a happier and better life. Communism is a much more serious claim. But every such claim is dangerous when it asserts itself to be sufficient as a source of life. So the church marches with the claim that it carries the banner of the one true God, the only source of life. The weapons of the church are the demand for justice for other men, the manifestation of the love of God in its own life, and the preaching of the gospel of forgiveness. It rejoices in every movement among men which strives for justice and the overthrow of ignorance, want, and disease. But it can only denounce every movement which claims to be worthy of man's ultimate concern or to be a source adequate to sustain man's life.

The Kingdom to Come

As each of us must acknowledge when we consider the world in which we live, God's kingdom does not extend to the whole of our life nor to the whole of the world. In fact, one must wonder whether it has made much progress over the centuries.

This fact raises questions concerning the meaning of Christ's teaching concerning the kingdom. Did he mean that it was coming in the future and that in him the first appearance of its coming was manifest to men? Or did he mean that it had come in him and that there would be a gradual spread until it was complete?

Most scholars agree that Christ understood that the kingdom was coming through him and would be complete in the future. "But if it is by the finger of God that I cast out demons, then the kingdom of God has come upon you" (Luke 11:20).

The expectation of an immediate return of Christ and the full establishment of the kingdom dominated the thinking of the early years of the church. As the years passed and the kingdom was not fully established, it became necessary to reevaluate this understanding.

In times of relative peace and prosperity the tendency has been to assume that the kingdom is here as we are in Christ, and that it is our responsibility to complete the work begun in Christ. In times of stress and catastrophe the emphasis shifts to an expectation of a final culmination and completion wrought by God.

Both of these views lose something of the fullness of the New Testament and of Luther. The kingdom is established in Christ and we are to find peace and joy now. The battle is not over in us, nor in the world, and we live under the mandate to fight on. Though we will advance the cause of Christ, the final conclusion will be accomplished by God and all that is imperfect will be made perfect. The warfare will cease and the victory of God will be established and apparent to all.

So the Christian rejoices in the kingdom which is present for him as he is in Christ. He seeks to advance this kingdom, where he grows through grace. But the hope of ultimate victory lies in a coming and conclusive act of God.

References and Resources

Aulén, Gustaf. *The Faith of the Christian Church*, Sections 36 and 51.

Heinecken, Martin J. *Basic Christian Teachings*, Chapter 10.

Kantonen, T. A. *The Christian Hope.* Philadelphia: Muhlenberg Press, 1954.

> *The whole of this brief book is a valuable resource for this chapter.*

See also:

Augsburg Confession: Article XVII.

Small Catechism: Second and Third Articles of the Creed and the Second Petition of the Lord's Prayer.

evangelical ethics 15

How does a man of Christ live a life of obedience to God under the pressures of a broken world? This will be the theme of this chapter, primarily as the problem is seen from the point of view of our relationships with others.

You shall not steal (Exodus 20:15).

I decided I wanted to live. Nothing else counted but that I wanted to live. I could have stolen from husband, child, parent, or friend, in order to accomplish this.... I would remain close to those who were too far gone and too weak to eat their meager rations of ersatz coffee or soup, and instead of pressing them to eat so that they might exist, I would eagerly take it from them and wolf it down if they gave the slightest evidence that the effort for them was too great.°

°Elie A. Cohen, *Human Behavior in the Concentration Camp* (New York: Norton, 1953), p. 136.

These are the words of a "cultured woman noted for her generosity and humanitarian interests" who found her values challenged by her experience in the Lensing concentration camp during the second world war. It makes a difference, doesn't it? But in what way? Does extreme need, a threat to life itself, set aside the ancient commandment against stealing?

The Sharpening of the Law

The New Testament has much to say about freedom and about justification by grace apart from the works of the Law. However, this should not hide from us the sharpening of the Law which occurs in the New Testament. One example will serve as a reminder of many others.

> "You have heard that it was said, 'An eye for an eye and a tooth for a tooth.' But I say to you, Do not resist one who is evil. But if any one strikes you on the right cheek, turn to him the other also..." (Matthew 5:38-39).

This sharpening of the Law is explicit in these words of Jesus:

> "Whoever then relaxes one of the least of these commandments and teaches men so, shall be called least in the kingdom of heaven; but he who does them and teaches them shall be called great in the kingdom of heaven. For I tell you, unless your righteousness exceeds that of the scribes and Pharisees, you will never enter the kingdom of heaven" (Matthew 5:19-20).

As we can see in the Epistles of the New Testament, the early church took the words of Jesus seriously. This is not to say that the first Christians were perfect, but even the casual reader will note the large place given in their writings to righteous living. Paul knew the tyrannical character of the Law, and he certainly proclaimed that Christ has fulfilled the Law, but he never argued that the standards of ethical behavior had been weakened — quite the opposite.

This extension of the requirements of Christian living is clear in Luther's explanation of the Fifth Commandment in the *Small Catechism:*

> We are to fear and love God so that we do not hurt our neighbor in any way, but help him in all his physical needs.

A literal understanding of the Old Testament commandment that one should not kill would judge few of us guilty. But when it is understood in the light of New Testament teaching and is extended to include the positive command that we befriend our neighbor in his every necessity, all of us are guilty to one degree or another. That we are in fact commanded to do these things is reiterated in Article VI of the *Augsburg Confession:*

> It is also taught among us that such faith should produce good fruits and good works and that we must do all such good works as God has commanded, but we should do them for God's sake and not place our trust in them as if thereby to merit favor before God....

The basic commandments of the New Testament are that we "love the Lord your God... and your neighbor as yourself" (Matthew 22:36-40). All of the specifications of the New Testament ethic are efforts to deduce what the command to love one's neighbor might mean in particular circumstances. But the specific circumstance never stands alone. It is always understood and applied within the larger context of love for one's neighbor. Neither are we to understand that having heard the specific, we are thereby empowered to do it. Christian ethical behavior is motivated by an interpersonal relationship in which the Christian responds to God's love for him, manifest in Jesus Christ.

Evangelical Freedom

> On another sabbath, when he entered the synagogue and taught, a man was there whose right hand was withered. And the scribes and the Pharisees watched him, to see whether

97

he would heal on the sabbath, so that they might find an accusation against him. But he knew their thoughts, and he said to the man who had the withered hand, "Come and stand here." And he rose and stood there. And Jesus said to them, "I ask you, is it lawful on the sabbath to do good or to do harm, to save life or to destroy it?" And he looked around on them all, and said to him, "Stretch out your hand" (Luke 6:6-10).

This passage presents us with a conflict. On the one hand, there was the ancient command to rest on the Sabbath. On the other hand, there was the immediate need of a man with a deformity. On what basis shall this conflict be resolved? We are forced to weigh a relationship to God which calls forth compassion against the specific command to rest on the Sabbath. For the Christian the matter can never be stated in as simple a form as: Did you or did you not do this thing? The question is whether or not what we do bears some reflection of God's way of dealing with us. This is the perspective from which the true nature of the problem is to be seen. This does not, however, allow us to ignore the ancient law concerning the Sabbath. It simply shows that in a certain circumstance we are free to make a decision which may not fulfill the letter of the ancient law but which may be a necessary response to God's love for us.

In a sense, this by itself does not describe freedom at all. It is quite logical to argue that the man who has a single command has a greater freedom: Do no labor on the Sabbath, regardless of the circumstances. This is not freedom from the Law; it is freedom from the anxiety of making a decision. However, as soon as the individual is asked to see a situation from the perspective of love, he faces the anxiety of multiple-choice. This is why the Christian concept of freedom is always linked with the witness to God's forgiveness.

Freedom and Forgiveness

It may be helpful to pursue the situation outlined in the opening paragraphs. Assume the common knowledge among concentration camp inmates that when a person can no longer fight for his food ration, he soon dies. Assume, also, that the apportioned ration was ultimately not sufficient to sustain life. A person who sees an inmate who is too weak to finish his food may, if able to think ethically at all, simply adhere to the basic commandment not to steal. Obey and accept the consequences. Or he may attempt to see the situation within the context of the New Testament command to love his neighbor. Then he must decide whether, if he feeds the weakened man, it will make a difference or simply waste the food. If he decides that it would be a waste of food, he must then decide whether to eat it himself or give it to another. In the event that he decides to try to serve the law of love, he faces the prospect of never knowing what might have been right in an absolute sense. This is why this freedom to make an ethical decision is really a freedom only if we make such decisions in the light of forgiveness.

Suppose that the woman in the example decided that this inmate would die anyway and so took the food. Was she right? Or might the other person have gained enough strength to return to the continued struggle for food? As Christians, it is our belief that her life would not ultimately rest upon the rightness of her decision but upon God's forgiveness, which allows her the freedom to decide.

Teaching and Practice

There are many doctrines of the church which large numbers of Christians do not understand. However, the church's teaching concerning ethics has been met not so much with misunderstanding as with unwillingness or inability to accept the teaching. That is, most of us prefer simple statements of what to do and what not to do. The responsibility for making a decision in a specific circumstance seems to be too great or to demand too much courage. We would rather be bound by laws. This is perhaps because we really prefer being right by the standard of specific laws to submitting to the law of love which means making hard decisions, the right or wrong of which are often unknown, and making our freedom contingent upon a genuine acceptance of God's forgiveness.

We have made no reference here to those who do not confess that the God of Jesus Christ is their ultimate concern. There are a wide range of ethical principles by which they may guide their behavior. It is the Christian who faces two interwoven traditions. The foundation is a body of basic commandments which both guide and condemn us. These guideposts are sacred and basic to human life. But breaking in upon these basic laws of God is the gospel of Jesus Christ with its declaration that God not only commands but also loves men. To be loved is to come under the impact of the will of the one who loves. The whole sound and feel of Christian ethics bears evidence to this. Our actions are the response to being loved, manifest in a new sensitivity to our neighbor and a desire to serve him. The result is certainly nothing less than what the law commands. But free in the assurance of forgiveness, the actions of the Christian can manifest a spirit which the Law can neither command nor produce.

References and Resources

Brunner, Emil. *The Divine Imperative.* Philadelphia: Westminster Press, 1947.
  See especially Chapter 14, "The Threefold Meaning of the Law."
Cohen, Elie A. *Human Behavior in the Concentration Camp.* New York: Norton, 1953.
Forell, George. *Faith Active in Love.* Minneapolis: Augsburg, 1954.

social ethics 10

The following two statements, formulated by the Convention of the United Lutheran Church in 1922 and 1960, illustrate the complexity of relating Christian teaching to social situations:

> The Convention declared its conviction:...(5) That the maintenance of great standing armies, and great navies, whether of the sea or of the air, not only imposes heavy and oppressive burdens on the people, and involves an appalling waste of the economic resources and the man power of the nations, but also constitutes a constant menace to the peace of the world. (1922 Convention, United Lutheran Church)

> We recognize that armaments are today a basic element in international diplomacy. Their possession in peace may serve to deter aggression. Their use in war for purposes of defense may be justified as a necessary evil in a sinful

world. . . . We are therefore convinced that the decision to have recourse to arms must be determined by the extent to which justice and freedom may be advanced. . . . We are persuaded that this dilemma will remain a burden of mankind through the foreseeable future and that decisions must be made humbly and responsibly as each new situation arises. . . . (1960 Convention, United Lutheran Church)

In 1922, it seemed clear to the convention delegates that nothing positive could be said about "large standing armies and great navies." In 1960, it seemed clear to the delegates that armaments were an element of diplomacy and could, in fact, serve the cause of peace and justice. One might conclude that the delegates just didn't know what they were talking about, in one case or the other, or that one convention upheld the ideal and the other chose the path of realism. There are, however, deeper factors involved in the production of the two statements. For one thing, Christian teaching provides no single approach to social problems. Equally important, the situations to which the conventions addressed themselves were radically different, even though both involved the matter of armaments.

Can the church and its members, from their particular standpoint as the people of God, relate themselves in any way to the changing patterns of social issues? The answer given in the past has run the whole gamut from indifference to social problems to assurance that the church can speak relevantly in quite specific ways. In order to find one's own answer to this question, there should be some consideration of biblical and historical precedents, the controlling thrust of the gospel, and the role of the institutional church in a democratic society.

In the Bible and the Confessions

One of the major New Testament statements concerning the Christian's relationship to political authority is given in Paul's Epistle to the Romans:

Let every person be subject to the governing authorities. For there is no authority except from God, and those that exist have been instituted by God. Therefore he who resists the authorities resists what God has appointed, and those who resist will incur judgment (Romans 13:1-2).

The First Epistle of Peter is equally clear:

Be subject for the Lord's sake to every human institution, whether it be to the emperor as supreme, or to governors as sent by him to punish those who do wrong and to praise those who do right (1 Peter 2:13-14).

The words of Jesus most often quoted in a discussion of church and society are "Render therefore to Caesar the things that are Caesar's, and to God the things that are God's" (Matthew 22:15-22). At first reading, this may seem to agree with Paul and Peter in assigning certain areas of authority to the state. But is this really what Paul and Peter meant and is it what Christ meant? There was a time in the first years of the church when Peter was called before the high priest in Jerusalem and accused of disobeying an order to cease preaching. His response was "We must obey God rather than men" (Acts 5:27-32). The Old Testament, too, contains a long history of civil disobedience on the part of the prophets. Jeremiah, for example, told Zedekiah, the king of Judah, that God himself would fight against him (Jeremiah 21:5). The prophet Amos said, "Jeroboam [the king of Israel] shall die by the sword, and Israel must go into exile away from his land" (Amos 7:11). When Amaziah, the priest of Bethel, told Amos he could not say such things in the king's sanctuary, Amos simply became more incisive in his condemnation of the Israelites' moral laxity and the evils of Jeroboam's reign.

It seems clear that the overall witness supports the God-given character of civil authority, but that this authority can be exercised in such a way that God is not properly served. In such a case Christians may, in God's name, disobey civil authority. This view is reflected in Article XVI of the *Augsberg Confession:*

It is taught among us that all government in the world and all

103

established rule and laws were instituted and ordained by God for the sake of good order, and that Christians may without sin occupy civil offices or serve as princes and judges, render decisions and pass sentence according to imperial and other existing laws, punish evildoers with the sword, engage in just wars, serve as soldiers, buy and sell, take required oaths, possess property, be married, etc. . . . But when commands of the civil authority cannot be obeyed without sin, we must obey God rather than men.

The difficulty with this position is in the practice of it. How do we decide when we should obey the civil authorities because they are instituted by God, and when we should disobey?

We have some historical precedent, of course. Some members of the early church were ordered to pay homage to Caesar as a god. They disobeyed because the order was diametrically opposed to their ultimate commitment to the God of Jesus Christ. On the other hand, there is some evidence that many Christians in Germany did not disobey Adolph Hitler because of their respect for the God-given authority of the state. Many pastors and priests in America during the 1960's were arrested for violating laws as they demonstrated against racial segregation. Did they rightly disobey? How shall we decide, in a particular instance, which course to follow?

The Force of the Gospel

The terror of being human is to be aware of one's own existence, to be haunted by the consequent questions of who we are and what our life is for, and to be constantly threatened by the crumbling of the answers which we have assumed to be adequate to these questions. The joy of the gospel is to know one's existence to be affirmed by God, and to find in him a meaning and purpose which sets us free of our anxiety. What God gives us is our life, but not in a biological sense alone. By loving us he provides the foundation which allows us to respond openly to him and to our fellowmen with love and freedom. God establishes our dignity and worth and destroys the anxiety about our existence which had held us captive.

104

It is the force of this message which should guide us in our relationship to society. We cannot offer other men this kind of ultimate freedom apart from their own experience of reconciliation to life in Jesus Christ. This is why the church has always insisted that its major task is the witness through which God calls men to himself. But our awareness of this ultimate freedom can sharpen our sensitivity to the ways in which men can begin to experience—hopefully through us or with our help—the meaning of the dignity and richness of human existence.

This means that whenever we face a social issue—whether it be economic, political, or in some other area—our primary questions must be: How can we best preserve and strengthen the full humanity of our neighbors? What will best protect them from the degradation of being discriminated against because they belong to a particular group? What can preserve them from arbitrary power?

Few things are more stifling to the development of moral responsibility and human dignity than being allowed to exercise arbitrary power against others or being subject to such power. What other things are important to the freedom and dignity of the human person? Among them are certainly the opportunity to work, adequate food and shelter, protection for the experience of love and authority within the family, some voice in the conduct of the economic and political affairs of the community, and access to whatever medical care is available. To work toward these goals for all men is certainly what it means to love one's neighbor.

The Church and Social Action

One of the problems which plagues the church in its approach to social issues is the division between some who would speak only the most idealistic insights of the gospel and those who insist that the church's pronouncements and actions be marked by realism. With respect to armaments, for example, some would say that since war is evil we must give up armaments. The response from others is that in a world of

105

power politics this would lead to even greater evils. Surely the truth is to be found in both positions. Of all people, Christians should know the power of sin and consequently should be prepared to engage in activity which, while not perfect according to Christian insight, allows a measure of progress at a particular point in history. At the same time, the church must acknowledge that there is a higher way which will always judge our partial steps.

But how shall we know how much can be accomplished now, and by what process should we go about making our decisions?

There is no certain way of knowing how much can be accomplished now. Christian men must make the best rational decisions they can. The situation itself will teach them much, and the Holy Spirit will prompt a right response. Here, too, we live by grace.

The process of decision-making will vary. Individual Christians, alive to God and to particular situations in their communities, will have to act on social questions. This may be by the ballot, by involvement in political parties, by taking part in demonstrations, or by other means. The various divisions of the Christian church will gather their best leadership to study social issues and to provide guidance for their members. In many situations the church will find it necessary and desirable to join forces with other elements of the community to accomplish objectives, even though others may have a motivation which differs from that of the church.

There will, of course, be differences of opinion within the church. There will be no permanently valid blueprints for social action. But we have received a great gift; our humanity has been restored. Our mission is to mediate this gift through the preaching of the Word and through action within the structures of society. Christians and the church will support the authority of the state when the state preserves and extends the dignity of man. Christians and the church will challenge the state when, in their judgment, the state acts to degrade and depersonalize men.

106

References and Resources

Aulén, Gustaf. *Church, Law, and Society.* New York: Scribner's, 1948.

Bennett, John C. *Christian Ethics and Social Policy.* New York: Scribner's, 1946.

Brunner, Emil. *Justice and the Social Order.* New York: Harper, 1945.

Letts, Harold (ed.). *Christian Social Responsibility,* Vol. I, Chapter 4; Vol. III.

Niebuhr, Reinhold. *Moral Man and Immoral Society.* New York: Scribner's, 1932.

Raughley, Ralph C., Jr. (ed.). *New Frontiers of Christianity.* New York: Association Press, 1962, pp. 63-80.

Temple, William. *Christianity and the Social Order.* New York: Penguin, 1942.

Williams, Daniel D. *What Present-Day Theologians Are Thinking,* Chapter 3.

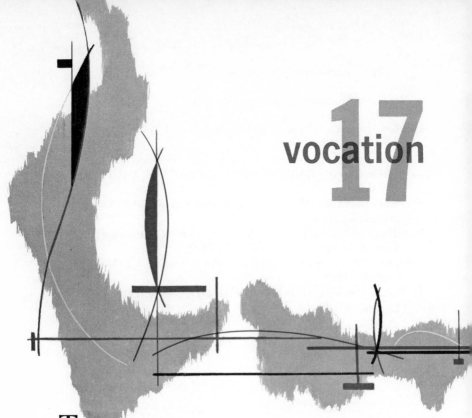

vocation 17

The Latin root for the word vocation means calling. But do we mean God's call to us to be his people? Or the station which we hold in life when we are called by God? Or that God calls us to a particular station in life? When we talk about "station in life," do we mean our occupation or something broader?

> Only, let every one lead the life which the Lord has assigned to him, and in which God has called him. This is my rule in all the churches. . . . Every one should remain in the state in which he was called. Were you a slave when called? Never mind. But if you can gain your freedom, avail yourself of the opportunity. For he who was called in the Lord as a slave is a freedman of the Lord. Likewise he who was free when called is a slave of Christ. You were bought with a price; do not become slaves of men. So, brethren, in whatever state

each was called, there let him remain with God (1 Corinthians 7:17-24).

This is a troublesome passage, but it provides a starting point for a discussion of the word vocation and its meaning for the Christian life. How is Paul using the term calling in this passage from Corinthians? And most important, perhaps, what is the relevance of all of this to our actual life?

Called to Be God's People

The New Testament uses the term calling primarily to indicate God's address to men. The first two sentences in the passage from Corinthians, in which the passage is used to indicate a man's position in life, is the one major exception. The following passage from the First Epistle of Peter is an example of the way in which the term is most often used:

> But you are a chosen race, a royal priesthood, a holy nation, God's own people, that you may declare the wonderful deeds of him who called you out of darkness into his marvelous light. Once you were no people but now you are God's people; once you had not received mercy but now you have received mercy (1 Peter 2:9-10).

This is also the sense in which the term is used in Philippians:

> I have not yet reached perfection, but I press on, hoping to take hold of that for which Christ once took hold of me. My friends, I do not reckon myself to have got hold of it yet. All I can say is this: forgetting what is behind me, and reaching out for that which lies ahead, I press towards the goal to win the prize which is God's call to the life above, in Christ Jesus (Philippians 3:12-14, New English Bible).*

Far from indicating a station in life or an occupation, these two passages have a quite different orientation. In the passage from Peter, it is a call out of darkness. In Philippians, it is a call to life above. Basically it is a call into a relationship with God through Jesus Christ, a call to the prodigal to return home. Any

*See also Hebrews 3:1; Ephesians 4:4.

109

other use of the term is derived from this. Those who are called into a new relationship with God become something new as a result. But to become and to be inevitably mean to do or to act in accordance with what we now are. This being, doing, and acting occur now, while we live in the midst of the world. Our calling to a new relationship with God demands some reflection on the station or position which we hold among men. Paul, in the passage from 1 Corinthians, moves easily from God's call to the station we held in life at the time that we were called. The next step in the development of the use of this term is to apply the term calling to the positions we occupy as people under the call of God. Therefore Paul and also the Reformers can speak of vocation both as God's call to us and the work or positions of the people whom God has called. These are the places and the ways in which God's call to us is manifest.

God's Calling and a Man's Station

God calls plumbers to be his people, but he does not call men to be plumbers. The man who is a plumber and who is called into a new relationship with God through Christ, manifests his calling in his work as a plumber. In a derivative way the plumber may bear witness that God called him to be a plumber, but he cannot state as a general proposition that God calls every man to whatever work he happens to be doing. This distinction is of some importance, since otherwise the general teaching that God is responsible for our every situation would destroy the importance of our choices and eliminate the moral responsibility which choice implies.

The one area of occupation which is most debated in this respect is the preaching of the gospel, largely because Paul speaks of himself as being called to be an apostle of Jesus Christ (Romans 1:1; 1 Corinthians 1:1; Galatians 1:15). Certainly the Old Testament prophets also felt that they had been called by God to fulfill a specific task. On the basis of the biblical witness and our own inclinations, we are generally

110

willing to distinguish between those who serve the office of the ministry and those who have other work. All men, we say, are called to be Christians. Some are specifically called as preachers. Others are not called to specific work, but should show the meaning of their new lives in whatever positions they find themselves.

One thing alone is a part of our common experience of God, that he calls us to new life in relationship to himself through Jesus Christ. This new life will be lived out in all the stations or positions which we occupy in our life in the world. Some of us also would bear witness that he has called us into these specific positions in the world for reasons which serve his own purpose and in ways which are beyond our knowing.

Affirmation of the World

The *Augsburg Confession* has some passages which are seldom quoted, but which have much to say about vocation. The following are two examples:

> ... The Gospel does not overthrow civil authority, the state, and marriage but requires that all these be kept as true orders of God and that everyone, each according to his own calling, manifest Christian love and genuine good works in his station of life. ... (Article XVI)

> It is also taught among us that man possesses some measure of freedom of the will which enables him to live an outwardly honorable life and to make choices among the things that reason comprehends. But without the grace, help, and activity of the Holy Spirit man is not capable of making himself acceptable to God. ... (Article XVIII)

Several things are either explicit or implicit in these passages. The first is an affirmation of the world and of the stations or positions which men hold in the world. Marriage is a legitimate estate for Christians. So also the position of ruler, judge, payer of taxes, collector of taxes, farmer, tradesman, or almost anything else. This positive statement is too often

111

hidden in our concern for worldliness and the negative connotations which we attach to the word secular.

The second thing to note is the affirmation of man's capacity for "civil righteousness" (the term used in the Latin text of Article XVIII of the *Augsburg Confession*), and of our freedom to make decisions on the basis of human reason. This teaching has also been hidden by our insistence that man is a sinner and by our suspicion of all human judgments. To teach that we can live honorably in the world and make decisions and choices on the basis of reason is also an affirmation of the world and our life within it.

The third thing to be noted is that while much that is positive is said about our life in the world, this is not meant to imply that what we do in the world will bring us a saving relationship with God.

The resultant picture is Luther's concept of the two kingdoms. On the one hand man lives in the world, affirms it, and holds positions within it. Here God is also at work, maintaining and serving his children in ways hidden to the eyes of the nonbeliever but nevertheless effective in serving his needs. On the other hand there is the kingdom of heaven, which is not so much a place as a restored relationship, in which human life is given its true meaning and foundation.

Life in the Two Kingdoms

The Christian man has a vocation in the sense that he is called by God into a new relationship with himself. He also has various stations or positions in this life in the world. The relationship between his calling by God and his stations in the world is indicated by Gustaf Wingren:

> He who does not have faith and, through faith, access to the heavenly kingdom, knows only different masks. He knows only the earth, where God appears solely as hidden behind his many masks: parents, rulers, neighbors, wives, children, etc. Without faith, a man cannot distinguish between God and his masks. . . .

112

Not being able to differentiate between God and his mask is the same as not being able to distinguish between the two kingdoms of earth and heaven. The stations and offices which are excluded from the heavenly kingdom remain inescapably in the earthly kingdom. Faithfulness in them benefits one's neighbor, who is the objective of the works required of man on earth.

A Christian despises nothing; he maintains a proper perspective in respect to all earthly glory by putting everything in its right place. In his affirmative response to his vocation he affirms the world whose totally relative character before God he has already recognized. As he looks upon the context of his earthly vocation, his thought is that this is not a world in which man can place his trust, but one in which he can serve.*

In summary, therefore, every man lives in the world, affirming its goodness by faithfulness to the offices and positions which he holds, making decisions which within the earthly frame are to be praised or condemned on the basis of whether they promote the well-being of men. The Christian is a man of the world who is called through Christ into a new relationship with his Creator. As a result of this experience (rebirth, salvation, reconciliation), the Christian understands both that his civil righteousness has not brought him to God and that, having been restored by God, his stations in the world are the ways by which he will knowingly serve his neighbor. Will he serve his neighbor better now that he has been restored to God? Surely it is God's desire that a man, having been set free from anxiety about the meaning of life, will have the capacity to love his neighbor with some new perception and depth.

References and Resources

Heiges, Donald. *The Christian's Calling.* Philadelphia: Muhlenberg Press, 1958.

Wingren, Gustaf. *Luther on Vocation.* Philadelphia: Muhlenberg Press, 1957.

*Gustaf Wingren, *Luther on Vocation* (Philadelphia: Muhlenberg Press, 1957), pp. 140-141.

sanctification 18

What happens in the life of a man after he becomes a Christian? In what sense is he sanctified, or holy, and in what ways does he grow in sanctification, or holiness of life? There is no easy answer to these questions, in part because the Bible itself seems to allow multiple interpretation.

> You know that he appeared to take away sins, and in him there is no sin. No one who abides in him sins; no one who sins has either seen him or known him. . . . No one born of God commits sin; for God's nature abides in him, and he cannot sin because he is born of God (1 John 3:5-6,9).°

> For I do not do the good I want, but the evil I do not want is what I do. . . . Wretched man that I am! Who will deliver me from this body of death? Thanks be to God through Jesus Christ our Lord! So then, I of myself serve the law of God

°See also Romans 6:11-12, 22; Ephesians 4:17-32; Galatians 5:24-25.

with my mind, but with my flesh I serve the law of sin (Romans 7:19,24-25).*

How can these two passages be reconciled? The writer of the First Epistle of John, speaking to Christians, says that they cannot sin. Paul, a Christian, says that he does sin. This is a question of considerable importance, and the effort to describe the "style of life" of the Christian deserves attention. Without pretending to have resolved all of the issues involved, it is at least possible to indicate what these issues are.

Sanctification and the Holy Spirit

The *Small Catechism* follows the tradition of linking the three sections of the Creed with the major acts of the Trinity. The third article, the confession of the Holy Spirit, is identified with sanctification. This is made clear in the explanation which Luther provides.

> I believe I cannot by my own understanding or effort believe in Jesus Christ my Lord, or come to him. But the Holy Spirit has called me through the Gospel, enlightened me with his gifts, and sanctified and kept me in true faith. In the same way he calls, gathers, enlightens, and sanctifies the whole Christian church on earth, and preserves it united with Jesus Christ in the one true faith.

This is fully consistent with Luther's understanding of the completeness of God's saving activity. It is not only that God has created us and restored us to himself in Jesus Christ, but Luther also understands the New Testament to teach that even our response, our faith, is God's act. Not only is God the revealer, himself revealed in Christ, but he is also the cause of our knowledge that this is so. It is God himself who allows his revelation to become our present experience — to become revealedness. But Luther does not mean to imply that, once called to the response of faith, we are free of divine activity. Our preservation in faith, our growth in the new relationship,

*See also 1 John 1:8; Philippians 3:7-11; Romans 3:19-26.

and our sanctification occur under the direction and through the power of God the Holy Spirit. This is indicated, for example, in the following passage from Article XX of the *Augsburg Confession*.

> When through faith the Holy Spirit is given, the heart is moved to do good works. Before that, when it is without the Holy Spirit, the heart is too weak.

This is a point of beginning. When we talk about sanctification we are not limited to a discussion of following the example of Jesus. As in every aspect of Christian teaching, we are still confronted by acts of God in which he manifests his lordship, not only calling us to faith, but daily guiding us in his ways. But we must face the question with which we began. In what way and to what extent does the Christian lead a different kind of life, or become holy?

Sanctification and Justification

There are at least three major ways of describing the relationship between justification (one's restoration to God) and sanctification (the quality of the life of the Christian).

The first is a perfectionist view, represented in the passage from 1 John 3 which was quoted at the beginning of the chapter. It should be said, of course, that even the writer of this epistle recognized that Christians do sin. For example, "If we say we have not sinned, we make him a liar, and his word is not in us" (1 John 1:10). Nevertheless, the admonition is that this is both unacceptable and unnecessary. It is inconceivable that a man who has been restored to God should again yield to the power of sin. If he does sin, he ought to be able to stop, and must do so. The conviction that the Christian *ought* to lead a new life runs through the whole New Testament. The perfectionist view of the new man asserts that he *can* do so. Some Christian denominations hold this view as a matter of doctrine.

The second approach is a progressive one. God has saved

us. We are restored to the true source of our being. Gradually, as we mature in faith and as we better understand God's will, we will grow in our capacity to do what he demands and expects. The power to grow in this way has a twofold source. On the one hand, the Holy Spirit guides and directs. On the other hand, man rallies his own will to move as the Spirit directs. In many respects, this view is the most attractive. It allows place for both God and man, and represents the kind of cooperation which exemplifies one of the traditional values of the American style of life. (Said the pious neighbor to the farmer, "God has done well by you." "Yes," said the farmer, "but you should have seen this field when God was doing it by himself.")

The third view, sometimes attributed to Luther,* is a more pessimistic one. The only righteousness or holiness which we have or can attain is not ours at all but is given to us by God through Christ. Even after our restoration to God, we do not do the perfect will of God or make any progress toward doing so. We are called holy, or saints, because God has covered us with the perfection of Christ. But apart from our righteousness *in Christ* we continue to sin and will continue to do so until God comes again and all things are made new. This third view is certainly represented in the passage from Romans with which the chapter begins. One result of such a view could be a passive attitude toward all forms of evil, whether in ourselves or in the world. If we cannot do what is right, and cannot grow in our capacity to do what is right, why make any effort?

Article VI of the *Augsburg Confession* suggests another approach, which breaks the pattern of the first three and provides a fresh understanding:

> It is also taught among us that such faith should produce good fruits and good works and that we must do all such good works as God has commanded, but we should do them for God's sake and not place our trust in them as if thereby to merit favor before God. For we receive forgiveness of sin

*Reinhold Niebuhr, *The Nature and Destiny of Man* (New York: Scribner's, 1945), II, pp. 184-198.

and righteousness through faith in Christ, as Christ himself says, "So you also, when you have done all that is commanded you, say, 'We are unworthy servants' " (Luke 17:10).

This is also said by Paul in his Epistle to the Philippians:

Not that I have already obtained [resurrection from the dead] or am already perfect; but I press on to make it my own, because Christ Jesus has made me his own. Brethren, I do not consider that I have made it my own; but one thing I do, forgetting what lies behind and straining forward to what lies ahead, I press on toward the goal for the prize of the upward call of God in Christ Jesus (Philippians 3:12-14).

In both of these passages three things are being said. First, that our salvation or restoration to God has nothing at all to do with our good life. Sinful men are restored by an act of God's grace. Second, that the Christian is under the command to live a new kind of life. More than that, the man who responds to the love of God wants desperately to lead a life pleasing to God. Third, that the Christian, perhaps more than any other, is either sharply aware of his failure to do so or proud of whatever success he has, which is a greater failure. Can there be progress in the way in which a man lives with his neighbors? Of course. But this fact does not dispel the tension between what he is and what he should be. This tension always remains, and we can live with it only because we live by daily repentance and forgiveness. But the forgiveness is in turn that which allows us to press on and to face again the tension of command and failure.

This is not the first view listed, because it does not allow true Christian perfection. It is not the second view, because it does not allow progress toward true holiness, even with divine help. It is not the third view, because it will not allow us to become passive toward the command of God and the desire to press on toward holiness. It is something else, a view which demands that the Christian live between the command and his own failure, trusting in God alone to provide peace and joy in the midst of the tension. If we allow some biblical authority

118

for this last understanding, what shall we then say about sanctification?

Sanctification and Acts of Devotion

Ultimately, sanctification must be described in terms of the quality of our relationship with God. As often as we reduce the Christian life to the question of right and wrong, just that often the Bible challenges the adequacy of this category of understanding. Obviously, right and wrong actions are an integral part of our relationship with God, but this emphasis upon morality is corrupting whenever it becomes central. The answer to our very existence, the source of our own meaning, is in God's love for us. These words do not describe a pattern of behavior; they describe the relationship of God with man. Sanctification describes the quality of this relationship. How pervasive is the impact of God's love upon our life? How deeply are we moved? How complete is our response? How regular and fruitful is the dialogue between man and God?

Analogy is dangerous, but how can we do without it? A young man and young woman confess love for one another at the time of their marriage, and they promise certain right actions. But the quality of the marriage is the continuing dialogue in which the mystery of the one is disclosed to the other and each grows in wonder at the depth of human love and loyalty. And there are rites and ceremonies which by themselves are nothing, but which become the outward and visible means by which they celebrate the relationship. By anniversaries and pictures, by mythologized stories of earlier events in their common life, by rings and songs and words used with special meanings, they rehearse their relationship and grow in faithfulness.

So also, at the heart of sanctification is the increasing depth of a man's relationship with God. The love of God is symbolized and rehearsed in the acts of God in Christ, and the witness to these acts is read and heard, sung in hymns and canticles, observed and celebrated in the festivals of the year. The daily

119

round of morning and evening prayer, the weekly round of confession and adoration, praise and thanksgiving, the coming to the Lord's table—these are the times of encounter and the instruments through which the Holy Spirit refreshes us and brings us into the presences of the Father. There certainly can be growth in our relationship with God. At the same time, the Christian does not say of this growth, "I am becoming more holy." He lives with the tension of the demand for total commitment, knowing that he is not totally committed. But the forgiveness of God cuts the Gordian knot and allows him to press forward with anticipation.

Sanctification and the Neighbor

The assertion that the quality of our relationship with God is central to the doctrine of sanctification does not eliminate growth in right relationships with the neighbor. But our relationship with our neighbor now becomes the place in which God also confronts us, revealing himself. Obviously, prayer at 7:00 A.M. and a business decision at 10:00 A.M. are not the same thing. But in each of these times and places God may call us to grow in our relationship with him. To say that this relationship is best fostered in one place or the other is to miss the wholeness of the Christian life.

There also certainly can be growth in right actions. But again, the Christian does not say of this growth, "I am becoming more holy." He lives with the tension of the demand for total commitment and the limited goodness of his actions. As with growth in his relationship with God, it is the forgiveness of God which cuts the Gordian knot, and allows him to press forward with joy.

Sanctification is the work of the Holy Spirit by which we are called to an ever-deepening relationship with God through acts of devotion and acts of service to our neighbor. Denying perfectability but growing in our relationship, we depend totally upon the grace of God. We praise him for growth, but we know that we live by grace, and not by growth.

References and Resources

Aulén, Gustaf. *The Faith of the Christian Church,* pp. 301-328.
Barth, Karl. *Dogmatics in Outline,* Chapters 21-23.
Orwell, George. *Animal Farm.* New York: Harcourt, Brace, 1954.

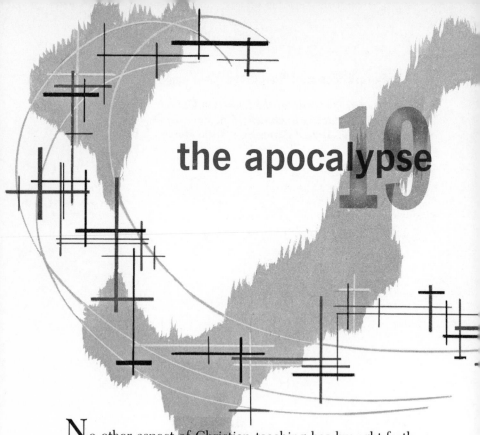

the apocalypse

N o other aspect of Christian teaching has brought forth as much speculation in times past, and perhaps no other teaching is as unappreciated in the modern church. Yet it must be acknowledged that the apocalypse was central in Christ's teaching. What was the content of this teaching, and what is its relevance for mature Christians in the twentieth century?

Then I saw a new heaven and a new earth; for the first heaven and the first earth had passed away, and the sea was no more. And I saw the holy city, new Jerusalem, coming down out of heaven from God, prepared as a bride adorned for her husband; and I heard a great voice from the throne saying, "Behold, the dwelling of God is with men. He will dwell with them, and they shall be his people, and God himself will be with them; he will wipe away every tear from their eyes, and death shall be no more, neither shall there be mourning nor crying nor pain any more, for the former things have passed away" (Revelation 21:1-4).

It is also taught among us that our Lord Jesus Christ will return on the last day for judgment and will raise up all the dead, to give eternal life and everlasting joy to believers and the elect but to condemn ungodly men and the devil to hell and eternal punishment (*Augsburg Confession,* Article XVII).

Here, in the poetry of Scripture and the prose of doctrine, we are confronted with the church's teaching concerning the apocalypse, the unveiling. "Eschatology," "parousia," and "last judgment" are terms which are closely associated with apocalypse, and all refer to a conclusive act of God which is yet to come. Eschatology is the study of those things which shall mark the end of time. Parousia refers to the return of Christ. The last judgment is a term indicating a major element of this act of God to come. Together, these terms indicate an event to come which shall be the end of all events in time, which shall unveil things hidden and bring men before the judgment seat of God.

When Will the End Come?

It should be kept in mind that there is a sense in which the end has already come in Jesus Christ. The old age has been fulfilled and the new age has begun.* But concurrent with this view is the teaching that God will break in again to complete the work begun in Christ. But when? The New Testament witness is that it will be soon, but that the exact time is not known.

> "Truly, I say to you, this generation will not pass away till all these things take place. Heaven and earth will pass away, but my words will not pass away.
> But of that day and hour no one knows, not even the angels of heaven, nor the Son, but the Father only" (Matthew 24:34-36).

*See Matthew 12:28; Luke 10:18; Luke 10:23-24; Matthew 11:2-6.

The teachings at the beginning of the chapter are both expressed in the parable of the ten virgins (Matthew 25:1-13). We must be prepared for the coming of the Bridegroom for it will be soon, but we can't know the exact moment. There are many signs of the coming end (Matthew 24), but there will still be false readings of the signs.

This announcement of the coming kingdom of God was present in the Old Testament, and is expressed in apocalyptic form in the Book of Daniel. The new element in Jesus' teaching was not just that it would come, but that he himself was its beginning (Mark 14:61-62). Much of Paul's advice is based on his expectation that the apocalypse was close at hand. This is why it made little difference whether they married or not. Why bother? The time was at hand when there would be no such thing as marriage. Some scholars feel that the kingdom parables in Mark may show some change from their original parable form when recorded by Matthew and Luke. The kingdom had not come, so the parables were redirected.

Elements of the End

The parousia, the return of Christ, is a major element in Christian apocalyptic. Again, we have a double concept. Christ is now among us and rules as the head of the church. At the same time, his rule is also challenged within the church. But there will be a time of unveiling when the rule of Christ will become manifest to all and the relationship of the Lord and his people will become perfectly realized.

The major passage in which Christ indicated his return is the following:

> "Are you the Christ, the Son of the Blessed?" And Jesus said, "I am; and you will see the Son of man sitting at the right hand of power, and coming with the clouds of heaven" (Mark 14:61-62).

This expectation is expressed by Paul with one word, "Maranatha," Our Lord, come! (1 Corinthians 16:22). The

Apostles' Creed expresses this expectation in the single phrase "... and is seated on the right hand of God, the Father Almighty, whence he shall come to judge the living and the dead."

It is difficult for us to know how large a place his return played in Jesus' own consciousness. It is clear that the early church expected his return and longed for it. Since the Christian's understanding of God and his reconciliation to him have been mediated through Christ, it is thoroughly consistent to expect that Christ, the revealer, will again be the mediator of our experience of God's concluding acts.

A second element of the apocalypse is an act of judgment. The Book of Revelation presents a detailed picture of this in the special language of apocalyptic, but Matthew also provides us with an image.

> "When the Son of man comes in his glory, and all the angels with him, then he will sit on his glorious throne. Before him will be gathered all the nations, and he will separate them one from another — as a shepherd separates the sheep from the goats, and he will place the sheep on the right hand, but the goats at the left" (Matthew 25:31-33).

Article XVII of the *Augsburg Confession,* printed at the beginning of this chapter, restates this same teaching.

Again we are confronted with a double image. It is not legitimate to ask whether our judgment occurs now or at the apocalypse. There is a witness to both in the New Testament. As Paul indicates, the man who tries to live by that which cannot give life suffers now the judgment of death (Romans 6:23). Judgment in this sense may not even be recognized, but the "sickness unto death," the anxiety concerning the foundation and meaning of our lives, is from a Christian perspective a judgment which every man, alienated from God, suffers. Judgment comes in an even sharper way for the Christian through confrontation with God's love in Jesus Christ. The experience of being unconditionally loved has as its product a painful awareness of one's own unrighteousness.

But this, too, is seen through Paul's dark glass. There shall come a time at the boundary between time and eternity when judgment shall be made. On what basis shall we be judged? Matthew 25 indicates one basis: What was the character of our life? What did we do? But the major basis emphasizes our reception of forgiveness.

> Then one of the elders addressed me, saying, "Who are these, clothed in white robes, and whence have they come?" I said to him, "Sir, you know." And he said to me, "These are they who have come out of the great tribulation; they have washed their robes and made them white in the blood of the Lamb" (Revelation 7:13-14).

But how can a loving God reject some men forever and ever? Such a question assumes more than Christian faith is able to say. In the first place, the gospel is not about God's rejection, but about his acceptance of men who are unworthy. It is also a gospel which proclaims with joy a God who will not destroy men's freedom to say "No," even to God. The question at the judgment is whether a man has accepted the loving forgiveness of God in Christ. Will the man who has refused God's gifts have another chance? This we do not know. We can only state what we know of God's intention and desire as revealed in Christ. Apocalyptic teaching declares, however, that there shall be an event, an unveiling, when each man will be confronted with the foundations of his existence and shall know the consequence.

What will be the signs of the end? When the gospel has been preached, when the Jews have been won, when the conflict between God and the hosts of darkness has reached its climax, then the end will come.* But everything which is said about the signs of the end specifies that we know neither the day nor the hour. We live between the temptation to count everything as a sign of the end and the temptation to be totally unconcerned because we cannot know when it will come. Once again, the Christian man lives by faith, trusting God to bring his kingdom when he will, but confident that the final victory of God is assured, whether it comes now or in some future age.

The Significance of This Teaching

Christian apocalyptic teaching has had little meaning for some Christians, not because it is objectionable in itself, but because they understand the balance of Christian teaching in a way which makes the apocalypse unimportant and unnecessary. If we can know God fully here in time; if we can be perfectly aware of the will of God; if we can grow satisfactorily in our relationship with God and in our capacity to do the will of God; if there is no tension between faith and doubt, between being saved yet continuing as sinner, between what God requires and what the world is — then there is little importance in a final act of God. In such a theology, the question of a final victory does not depend upon a final act of God, but upon the determination of a man to "take Christianity really seriously as a way of life, and to do his best to fulfill its requirements. When a man has done his best, that's it."

But when Christianity is understood as a cosmic struggle between the Creator and all that he has created; when we are torn by both knowing God and not knowing him; when we are confronted by the demand for a life grounded in his love, yet know our life to be taken from other sources; when we live under the demand to love our neighbor, but live also in the knowledge of our mixed motivations; when we know something of the possibilities for human life on the earth, and the sickness of this life — then the promise of a consummation, an apocalypse, is a source of hope and joy. It announces that in spite of the brokenness of our lives, the evil we have experienced, the defeats which God has suffered in his struggle, God shall yet reign supreme and bring all things to perfection.

... The eschatological framework of the teaching of Jesus is of permanent significance because it provides a symbol of the truth that history finds its consummation in him. We do not know how many civilizations will rise and fall before the end

°Matthew 24; Revelation 6:12-17; Revelation 7.

127

of the historic process on this planet.... But this we believe: that history has its meaning in the rule of the God and Father of our Lord Jesus Christ. God judges the world through him.... No matter how rebellious the sons of men remain, the victory of God is assured by his free act. He who created in the beginning will determine the consummation, for all life is in his hands. Hence we must take these long polysyllables out of the vocabulary of biblical specialists and let a true "Hallelujah Chorus" ring out in our own time; "The kingdom of the world has become the kingdom of our Lord and of his Christ, and he shall reign for ever and ever" (Revelation 11:15).*

References and Resources

Bornkamm, Günther. *Jesus of Nazareth.* New York: Harper, 1960.
Kantonen, T. A. *The Christian Hope.* Philadelphia: Muhlenberg Press, 1954.
   This book is a major resource for this chapter.

*Clarence T. Craig, *Interpreter's Bible* (New York: Abingdon-Cokesbury, 1951), VII, p. 154. By permission.